C000212092

WORDS
OF A
FEATHER

WORDS
OF A
FEATHER

An Etymological
Exploration of
Astonishing Word Pairs

Graeme Donald

metro

Published by Metro Publishing,
an imprint of John Blake Publishing Ltd,
3 Bramber Court, 2 Bramber Road,
London W14 9PB, England

www.johnblakebooks.com

www.facebook.com/johnblakebooks

twitter.com/jblakebooks

This edition published in 2015

ISBN: 978 1 78418 814 6

British Library Cataloguing-in-Publication Data:

A catalogue record for this book is available from the British Library.

Design by www.envydesign.co.uk

Printed in Great Britain by CPI Group (UK) Ltd

1 3 5 7 9 10 8 6 4 2

© Text copyright Graeme Donald 2015

The right of Graeme Donald to be identified as the author of this work has been
asserted by him in accordance with the Copyright, Designs and Patents Act 1988.

Papers used by John Blake Publishing are natural, recyclable products made from
wood grown in sustainable forests. The manufacturing processes conform to the
environmental regulations of the country of origin.

Every attempt has been made to contact the relevant copyright-holders, but some
were unobtainable. We would be grateful if the appropriate people could contact us.

For my wife, Rhona; definitely the
best pairing I ever managed.

INTRODUCTION

Some books are the result of a straightforward idea or chain of thought but *Words of a Feather* came from way out in left-field while digging into the family history of Al Capone to see if it was true that his older brother, Vinnie, had been a Federal Prohibition Agent. Not only had Vinnie been such an Agent but he had also worked on President Calvin Coolidge's security detail and been a Justice of the Peace. It also turned out that Al Capone was the driving force behind the imposition of the very first 'sell-by' dates on milk but that, as they say, is another story. This book was born of my noticing that 'Capone' was the Italian for 'capon', leaving the name of the hairy-scary gangster translating as Mr Castrated Chicken – and that got me thinking about hidden links between other words.

Furthermore, while rooting out the etymological links between words that, at first glance, appeared to have nothing to do with each other, I kept tripping over snippets of social and general history surrounding the origins of certain words. While checking out the connections between 'franchise' and 'frankfurter', for example, the mind made the obvious link (no pun intended) to 'hot dog' and a search into the precise origins of that nickname revealed the Germans to have been dog-eaters until the sale of such meat was banned in that country in 1986. I was already aware that every road, bridge and tunnel granting access to Switzerland stands mined and ready to blow at the flick of a switch, but I did not know that the Swiss are still enthusiastic devourers of both dogs and cats. That *did* come as a bit of a surprise.

Some manage to delve into the etymology of English with a straight face but I find it hard to discuss 'pumpernickel' meaning the devil-farter or the fact that 'knickers' is the Dutch for children's playing marbles without a wry smile. So, in the pages that follow I hope you will not only find the etymological links fascinating but also be able to laugh at the history of our language, which is anything but po-faced.

ACHIEVE and HANDKERCHIEF

Gladiators were the superstars of their day and death in the arena not anything like as frequent or inevitable as depicted in sword-and-sandal epics. The gladiator was simply too valuable an asset to be squandered in such manner; any school that lost half of its fighters at every games would soon have been out of business. That said, the debate as to the precise nature of thumb-signals used by the crowd at gladiatorial games continues but the general presumption that thumbs up meant 'let him live' and that thumbs down called for the vanquished to be killed is almost certainly wide of the mark.

There are ancient references to 'pollice verso', turned thumb, but no indication as to the direction. The bulk of opinion today seems to favour the notion that thumbs down meant drop the weapon and let him live as did the gesture of hiding the right thumb in the clenched fist of the left; death would be called for by a self-stabbing with the thumb to the chest.

What is known is that the mob would bay, 'Ad caput (venire)', literally 'bring it to a head' but used in the sense of 'finish it off'. With death in the arena regarded by the mob as the most entertaining outcome, Early French, building on its own 'chef', meaning head, took this original Latin expression to create the verb 'aschever', to bring matters to a successful conclusion, and then invented the antonym 'meschever', which basically meant 'to make a mess of things'. English adopted these two in the forms of 'achieve' and 'mischief', with the former still retaining its original gladiatorial overtones in certain contexts, as seen in Shakespeare's *Henry V*, in which the eponymous character says, 'Bid them achieve me and then sell my bones' (Act 4, Scene 3).

Now swept to obscurity by disposables, the humble 'hankie' began life as an ornate head covering – not unlike the Spanish mantilla – carried by women wishing to indicate a modest demeanour. First called in French a 'couvre-chef', or head covering, this entered English in the late 1200s as 'kerchief', but within a hundred years men too were wafting increasingly ornate lace kerchiefs in displays of flamboyance and ostentation, which attracted the inclusion of 'hand'. Far too expensive to blow your nose on, the handkerchief was the must-have iPad of its day, with Henry IV paying over 2,000 francs for one gold-embroidered hankie for his mistress.

Outlandish styles and shapes were curtailed in 1785, when

King Louis XVI of France banned the production of anything but square hankies. It took the introduction of snuff to simplify the accessory and bring it to its modern use: as people jack-knifed about the court in paroxysms of sneezing after shoving the new powder up their noses, the folly of blowing tobacco-stained mucus onto something so expensive started the drive towards increasingly plain and sturdy forms.

Incidentally, the practised snuff-taker only ever faked having to sneeze, in order to excuse himself from an embarrassing or boring situation, hence 'not to be sneezed at', as said about anything of genuine interest.

AFTERMATH and MOW

It is strange that 'aftermath' is now only used with negative overtones – the aftermath of war, or whatever – for it originally presented as 'aftermowth', a cognate of 'mow', and described the fresh growth that sprang up after the initial cutting of a meadow.

AJAR and CHARCOAL

The Middle English 'char' or 'charr' denoted a turn, so the door that stands neither open nor shut but halfway through its turn, is 'achar' or 'ajar'. The 'charlady' does a turn of work, concentrating on her 'chores', and wood that is burnt to such a state that it looks like it has been turned into coal is 'charcoal'.

Charing Cross in London is said to come from the French 'Chère Reine', or Dear Queen, after Edward I erected a cross there in the early 1290s to honour his departed wife, Eleanor of Castile. But although he was undoubtedly French-speaking – our first English-speaking king was Henry IV – the area was already known as Charing for its location on a bend, or turn, in the Thames.

ALBATROSS and ALCATRAZ

The relationship between these two terms involves a chain of misunderstanding and error leading back to the Arabic 'al qadus', water bucket. This term was originally used of the pelican in reference to its capacious pouch, but when it moved into Spanish and Portuguese as 'alcatraz' it was applied indiscriminately to the pelican, the albatross, the cormorant and the frigate bird. When the term arrived in 1680s English as 'algatrosse' it was misdirected at the large wandering bird, and, due to an assumption that the Latin 'albus', white, must somehow be involved, the spelling was altered to 'albatross'. When early Spanish explorers came across the now-infamous island in San Francisco Bay, they named it Alcatraz due to its flourishing colony of pelicans.

One cannot leave the subject of Alcatraz and birds without stating that Robert Stroud, the so-called Birdman of Alcatraz, never kept a single bird throughout his entire time on The Rock.

AMAZON and AMAZON and AMAZON

The three common but disparate senses of 'Amazon' – a Xena-like warrior of Greek mythology, a mighty river, and the online trader – all are inexorably linked.

When applied to lusty-limbed female warriors, the term has

excited all forms of conjecture, as one might imagine, with various scholars favouring the notion that the term was born of the Greek 'a mazos', without breast, as female offspring might have had the right breast cauterised at birth to make for more efficient archery in later life. However, women today excel at archery without recourse to such drastic measures, and no ancient image of the Amazons shows them to be thus mutilated.

There have been other suggestions but, as pointed out by the eminent etymologist Eric Partridge, there seems little reason to look beyond the Old Persian 'hamazon', a warrior. The Greeks and the Persians were forever at each other's throats and there is plenty of evidence of female Persian warriors on whom the Greeks could have built their legend. The female cavalry of Sassanid Persia (226–651) was widely and rightly feared, and, although they were around too late in the day to form the foundation of Amazons per se, these units could well have been followers of earlier female brigades. Who knows?

The Spanish expedition into South America in 1541, led by Gonzalo Pizarro and Francisco de Orellana, laboured under two linguistic misunderstandings. Inspired by the tales of El Dorado brought back by the 1500 expedition under Pinzón, Orellana went in search of what he imagined to be a golden city, whereas El Dorado had in a fact been a man covered in gold dust as part of a religious ritual. When Orellana reached the river referred to as the Amassona (Boat-Smasher) by the local Tupi, his mind immediately filled with images of naked female warriors along its banks, prompting him to alter the spelling.

5

In 1994, and inspired by 'abracadabra', Jeff Bezos founded his online trading company, Cadabra, but, tired of jokes and the pun on 'cadaver', he changed its name to Amazon the following year, imagining (with great perspicacity as it turned out) a mighty outpouring of merchandise.

AMBIDEXTROUS and DEXTROSE

The prejudice against left-handed people is ancient: in Latin 'dexter' meant of or pertaining to the right-hand side while 'sinister' meant to the left. 'Ambidextrous' was coined for those with equal 'dexterity' in both hands, and dextrose got its name because it always polarises light to the right in spectroscopy. This theme continues through the French 'adroit', to the right, which English adopted to mean capable, clever and able, and 'maladroit', that prefix meaning wrongly or badly, to denote those considered clumsy or inept. The straightforward French 'gauche', left, was also adopted for those considered socially inept.

The use of left and right in the political context was established by the seating arrangements of the French Estates General, which opened in 1789, with the nobility supporting the monarch being seated to the right with the rabble determined to wrest control from the elite being relegated to the left; the addition of 'wing' would be made in the nineteenth century. 'Sinister' likely took on its dark overtones through right-handed swordsmen having to face a 'southpaw' who, presenting every move in reverse, made for a 'sinister' opponent. The open stone staircases in castles and keeps traditionally spiralled up anti-clockwise so that invaders, likely to be right-handed, would have their sword arm impeded by the wall while the defenders had full sweep. The only exception to this rule is seen in Ferniehirst Castle near Jedburgh in Scotland, ancient home of the predominantly left-handed Kerr clan, whose spiral stairs run clockwise.

AMBULANCE and AMBITION

Both ultimately derive from the Latin 'ambulare', to walk, this in turn producing a second Latin term, 'ambitus', to walk around in a circle; 'ambient', as descriptive of the encircling environment, is therefore an allied term.

It was Baron Larrey, Napoleon's surgeon-in-chief, who invented the 'hospital ambulant', or walking hospital: medical teams with hooded litters, who walked about the battlefield, doing what they could on site and removing the more seriously wounded. By 1796, during Napoleon's Italian campaign, these walking units had been replaced by a more comprehensive deployment of horse-drawn carriages that were given the nonsensical name of 'ambulants volants', or flying walkers. Ignorant of the fact that the first element of that construction was in fact a plural, English adopted it in the form of 'ambulance'.

As for 'ambition', this was born of aspiring Roman politicians putting themselves about in the forum, pressing the flesh in an effort to drum up votes. The colour of the hem of one's toga indicated one's rank or station in society, so, to show the people he was 'one of them', the ambitious aspirant went 'candidatus', or dressed in white, hence 'candidate'. And we still fall for that

7

one! It was no better in Ancient Greece, where 'idiotes' described a private individual – a voter, in other words.

AMMONIA and TUTANKHAMUN

The Ancient Egyptians revered a deity called Ammon, Amon or Amun, whose temple at Siwa in what is now the Libyan Desert attracted droves of pilgrims. Staying for days at a time, the pilgrims tethered their transport in the nearby 'camel park'. Over the centuries, thousands of gallons of camel urine soaked into the sand; when the Romans turned up in 106 BC to dig out the foundations for a new fort, they uncovered large and foul-smelling crystals that were sent back to Rome for examination. The new discovery was named 'ammonia' for the place where it had been found. Once alerted to the cleansing power of ammonia, the Roman Empire began collecting urine – human and animal – for use in laundry and, believe it or not, oral hygiene; allowed to 'ferment' in large jars, urine was the first 'toothpaste'.

As for King Tut, his name meant 'The Living Image of Amon'; contrary to the popular presentation of the name, the accepted form in Egypt during his brief reign was Ammon-tut-Ankh, as the name of the god had to take precedence. To dispel another myth about the pharaoh, stories of a curse that befell those who desecrated his tomb are but press-fuelled fantasy. There was no curse inscribed anywhere on or in the tomb, and all involved in the plundering of the tomb under Egyptologist Howard Carter in 1922 lived, on average, for a further twenty-five years.

APOCALYPSE and CALYPSO

The shared root here is the Greek 'apokaluptein', to uncover or reveal, and the antonymic 'kaluptein', to hide or conceal.

A close cognate of 'apocryphal', denoting tales with hidden moral points, 'Apocalypse' first saw service in English as an alternative name for the last book of the New Testament, formally entitled the Revelation of St John the Divine. Penned by John of Patmos, this contains some pretty gruesome images – including the Four Horsemen who appear as harbingers of the Last Judgement – and fire-and-brimstone preachers ranting about the Armageddon of which the text made so much caused the term to shift to its present meaning.

As for 'calypso', the word was for many centuries primarily known as the name of the nymph-queen of the hidden island of Ogygia, who bewitched Odysseus to delay his return home from the Trojan Wars in Homer's *Odyssey*. Or at least that's what he told his wife. In more recent times it was applied to the songs of seventeenth-century slaves in the Caribbean, who, singing in a mixture of Creole and their own native tongues, hid in their songs bawdy and ridiculing references to their oppressors.

The 'crypt', in which the occupant is hidden from view, and the 'cryptic' crossword are also allied terms, as is the more remote relative 'grotto'.

ASSASSIN and HASHISH

Sometime around 1080, Hassan ibn-al-Sabbah, the 'Old Man of the Mountains', a childhood friend of Omar Khayyam, began sending forth his demented minions from his mountain fortress at Alamut in Persia to kill any Muslims opposed to his own version of 'the truth'. So no change in that neck of the woods over the last thousand years, then.

Eight years later the First Crusade landed on Hassan's doorstep, providing him with an endless supply of infidels to slay. Those who survived his attentions brought home tales of Muslim fanatics called the Hashisheen, or the hashish-eaters, who, allegedly out of their heads on said drug, would embark on frenzied killing sprees. That 'assassin' is derived from 'Hashisheen' is beyond dispute but not so the killers' use of the drug.

First mention of Hassan's minions using drugs comes from that old charlatan Marco Polo, who claimed to have visited Alamut in 1273 and come out alive. He tells of an induction ceremony during which recruits were given a sneak preview of the paradise that supposedly awaits all martyrs. They were, according to Polo, drugged up to the eyeballs and led to a dressed scene, complete with the scanty-pantied houri, or doe-eyed virgins, who allegedly stand ready to attend to all the needs and desires of dead martyrs. Trouble is that Polo writes of a potion that knocks the recruits senseless for days, which sounds nothing like hashish. But Polo cannot be regarded as a reliable source in that he likely got no further than Turkey, where he picked other travellers' brains about China. For one thing, he knew nothing of the Great Wall of China, which would have been a bit difficult for him to miss, if, as he claimed, he was dispatched hither and yon on the orders of Kublai Khan, who, in keeping with all other contemporary accounts, records nothing of any Venetian at his court.

'Hashisheen' has for centuries been employed metaphorically in Arab slang for any troublemaker or disruptive person, whether they take drugs or not. And it must be said that the followers of Hassan, although murderous terrorists, were Muslim fundamentalists and thus unlikely in the extreme to have taken drugs of any kind. In Edward Burman's *The Assassins: Holy Killers of Islam* (1987) the author explains that scholastic investigation into the cult has established that the attribution of the epithet 'hashish-eater' or 'hashish-taker' to Hassan's followers is a misnomer cooked up by the enemies of the Isma'ilis and, shunned by most Moslem chroniclers of the day, was only ever applied in the pejorative sense of 'enemies' or 'disreputable people'. He goes on to state that there is no mention of hashish in any contemporary chronicles, not even in the library at Alamut.

ATLAS and ATLANTIC

Early navigators had a problem: while their charts showed the earth as flat, their ships were in fact moving across a sphere, which called for complicated correctional calculations. Finally, in 1569, the Flemish cartographer Gerardus Mercator produced maps presenting the world as a flat plane, with the meridians parallel, but avoiding distortions to navigational routes. This made the navigator's job 'plane sailing' (not 'plain sailing').

Determined to have a suitably impressive frontispiece for his first book of these new-format maps, Mercator opted for the popular image of the Titan, Atlas, supporting the world on his back, after which the demi-god's name was applied to any collection of charts or maps. Unfortunately Mercator had misremembered his Greek mythology; Atlas's punishment for waging war on Olympus was not to carry the world but to support the heavens for eternity. He was transformed into rock so that he could perform this feat, and the Atlas Mountains were believed to be his petrified remains; the waters they overlook were called the 'Atlantic' Ocean.

ATTORNEY and TOURNAMENT

The Latin 'tornare', to turn, moved into French as 'tourner', which produced 'tourney', the forerunner of the knightly 'tournament'. With his weapon in one hand and a shield in the other, the rider could not hold the reins, so paramount was his ability to turn or manoeuvre his horse with signals from the knees. The 'attorney' is simply the person to whom you turn over your affairs.

'Tourniquet' is perhaps an obvious cognate but less so the 'turnip', which was named for its being a nepe or neep that looked as if it had been turned on a lathe. 'Turncoat' is first noted in the sixteenth century, which is long before soldiers had uniforms or even coats, so all the stories claiming that the word derives from deserters turning their coats inside out to hide their previous allegiance are spurious: how could cloth be dyed to show a different colour on each side? In such times, when only the rich had coats that were lined, a turncoat was one that was old and stained and thus turned inside out to 'show a different face' to the world.

Although 'tornado' properly derives from the Latin 'tonare', to thunder, after passing through Spanish it got confused with 'tornar', the Spanish cognate of the Latin 'tornare', to give a meaning of the turning wind, which, at the end of the day, is a pretty fair description. But as for the gastronomic 'tournedos', these present a mystery. As 'turncoat' now denotes a coward, so 'tournedos', with a basic meaning of turning your back (French 'dos') on something or someone, likewise referred to a coward in sixteenth-century French. How it made the leap to the table of the rich is anyone's guess. But beside being cognate to both terms in the heading, 'tournedos' is also cognate to the 'dosser' who is always flopped on his back, the paper-filled 'dossier' with a profile like a bent back, and the American country-dancing cry of 'do-si-do', calling on the participants to turn back-to-back.

ATTIC and ATHENS

Both Athens and Attica, the region in which the city stands, take their names from the goddess Athena, with 'Athens' and 'Attic' once broadly interchangeable. Before classical architecture was swept away by the upstart Gothic style, the triangular roof-supporting wall to the front of a building was always decorated with Grecian figures, so the void behind it was termed the 'attic'.

It is also worth noting that 'salt' in ancient times could also denote wit or wisdom, probably through the notion that such mental attributes added 'flavour' to the conversation, with Attic salt reckoned to be the best. The prudent were counselled to take what they were told 'cum grano salis', or with a grain of (Attic) salt – advice worth heeding to this day.

BANDIT and BANAL

The Old English 'bannan', to proclaim, is responsible for these and other allied terms such as 'banner', the wedding 'banns' and 'abandon'.

Proclamations were issued to 'banish' the unruly from the rest of society, thereby condemning them to live the life of a 'bandit', and, should such people tire of their status, they could always surrender or 'abandon' themselves to the mercy of the law. Forthcoming nuptials were announced by 'banns' to give objectors time to come forward and present their grievance, while feudal lords could issue banns at will to press the local serfs into servitude. Once in his 'employ', the lives they led were marked by drudgery and were thus 'banal'.

Although not etymologically linked, such servitude was also

known in Middle English as 'daunger', later 'danger', and, with the lords holding sway over life or death for those 'in their danger', that term shifted to describe peril in general.

BANKRUPT and BANQUET

If a medieval Italian moneylender became insolvent, city officials would come to the marketplace and, to signify such to all and sundry, smash up his trading counter with hammers; he was then declared 'banca rotto', broken bench. 'Charabanc' is an allied term that simply means a cart with benches.

As for 'banquet', this did not originally describe a sumptuous meal but rather a running buffet or snack that was laid out on a bench in a room other than the main dining hall, for guests in a prestigious residence to pick at as they chose. Sometimes a banquet was laid on as a final course to allow servants time to clear the main hall for the guests to cut a gavotte or two. For lesser mortals staying at the local inn, the equivalent was cold mutton and bread left out on a plank and trestles, hence 'bed and board', and it was doubtless the gulf between the standard of the two offerings that caused 'banquet' to shift in meaning.

BATMAN and BASTARD

Both owe existence to the old muleteers' packsaddle, known in English as a 'bat' and in French as a 'bast'.

In the first and military sense, the 'batman' was an officer's aide whose duty it was to pack his master's possessions in preparation for a campaign, and then to walk beside the mule to protect said items from the sticky fingers of the camp-followers who traipsed along with the baggage train behind any army on the move. Obviously this included ladies of a certain profession, hence 'old bag' or 'baggage' as an insult.

The use of 'bastard' for illegitimate issue arose from the fact that the packsaddle served as the muleteer's bed while he was on the trail; the assumption was that a child conceived in such circumstances was unlikely to be the product of a sanctified union. But it should be mentioned here that 'bastard' was not always an insult; there was a definite pecking order in bastardry.

To be the bastard of a king or noble was an honour, with royal bastards often given the surname Fitzroy (Son of the King). Appearing as a character in Shaw's *Saint Joan* (1924), Dunois, Bastard of (the Duke of) Orleans, would routinely have himself so announced in real life, while William the Conqueror was at home respectfully known as Le Grand Bâtard de Normandie, the illegitimate issue of Duke Robert 'the Devil' and a commoner called Harlette, who is often wrongly cited as the etymological inspiration for 'harlot'. Family reunions must indeed have been colourful events.

BEDLAM and BETHLEHEM

Bethlehem, which translates as 'House of Food', has always held great significance in Christianity; as far back as 1247, the Priory of the New Order of the Star of Bethlehem was founded as one of the first major religious institutions of London. By the fourteenth century, when the priory began to take in the abandoned insane, its name was commonly abbreviated to 'Bethlem' or 'Bedlam'. By the seventeenth century, the site was a rallying point for prostitutes and petty criminals and a favourite of Londoners who, for a few coppers admittance, could spend the day goading the inmates to the point of hysteria. Until it was moved from Moorfields to St George's Fields in south-east London in 1815, where it still exists as Bethlem Royal Hospital, Bedlam was infamous for its cruelty and the abusive nature of its regime, rendering its very name a synonym for utter chaos.

BEGGAR and BEGUINE

Prominent throughout medieval Europe were the Beghards, a mendicant movement of religious liberals who, although clad as friars or monks, took no vows, followed no rules and seem to have indulged in most earthly pleasures. Funding this enviable lifestyle by panhandling from town to town, the scepticism with which they were regarded by the average man-in-the-midden of early-thirteenth-century France led him to use the order's name for any scrounger. This usage quickly altered in French to 'begart' or 'begard', which arrived in English in 1225 as 'beggar'.

The parallel 'order' for women was that of the Beguines, who likewise seem to have enjoyed life to the full. Like the Beghards the Beguines took no vows, they did not have to observe any of the irksome rules of poverty and chastity, the better-heeled Beguine could be attended by her servants and many seem to have been what one might call 'party-animals'. There were also strong suspicions that many Beguinages were hotbeds of Sapphic practice. Be that true or not, still in present French to have 'le béguin' for someone means to view them with pronounced lust; the name of the now-sadly-lapsed order doubtless also has something to do with the name of the sultry dance.

BERSERK and SEASHORE

Taking their name from the Old Norse 'berr serkr', a bearskin shirt, the Berserkers were a clique of drug-crazed Viking warriors infamous for their outlandish behaviour both on and off the battlefield. Invariably in a state of advanced psychosis through ingesting fly agaric, a species of 'magic mushroom', they would charge into the fray, clad in their bearskin shirts, howling like wolves in their homicidal frenzy. Their antics were first described in *The Pirate* (1822) by Sir Walter Scott, and by the 1860s the term was appearing in metaphorical usage. Sixteenth-century European invaders of Malaysia were met with similar tactics employed by the tribesmen, who called their frenzy 'amok', whence 'to run amok'.

Both the 'shirt' (Old English 'serc') and the 'skirt' are garments cut to size (Old English 'sceran', to cut, a cognate of the Old Norse 'serk'); the association is perhaps clearer in the Scottish 'sark', as in *Cutty Sark*, the boat named after the short-shirt-wearing witch in Burns's 'Tam o' Shanter'. This sense of cutting continues through the 'share' that is cut from the main, the lamb that is 'shorn' and the 'shore' that cuts the sea from the land.

'Skor' was Old Norse for an incision so when counting sheep

out of a field, or whatever, the tally was marked on a counting-stick, which was 'scored' across its surface with a line at each batch of twenty, hence our lifespan of 'three-score and ten' – if we are lucky. Sporting scores were also kept on tally-sticks by means of scratches and incisions, with close of play marked by a deep incision or nick, whence 'in the nick of time'. The more complicated the deal being recorded the bigger the stick, hence 'stocks' as in stocks and shares. The same term as the heavy wooden stocks used to display miscreants in the marketplace, these cumbersome records presented a considerable storage problem and, on 16 October 1834, some lunatic (actually the Clerk of Works) decided to burn in the stoves in the basement of the House of Lords all the old stocks and tally-sticks which had been used by The Exchequer until as recently as 1826. So was started the fire that burned down the old Palace of Westminster.

BLAZER and BELARUS

The Old English 'blas', white, accounts for the white mark, or 'blaze', on a horse's forehead, as indeed it does for the 'trailblazer' who marks his new trail by hacking off bark from trees to expose the white wood underneath. The remote relative of 'belyj' in Old Bulgarian also produced Byelorussia (now 'Belarus'), meaning White Russia, in allusion to the traditional costume of that area.

Through association with white heat and things 'blazing', 1830s American slang used 'blazer' of anything or anyone outstanding, the term transferring to the highly coloured and conspicuous blazer as first worn by American college sporting teams. By the 1880s both the jacket and the term had been adopted by the boating fraternity of Henley and Oxbridge.

BLOOMERS and BLOOMER

Although many sources lay the dubious honour of having named the former at the undeserving feet of American women's rights campaigner Amelia Jenks Bloomer, the so-called 'bloomer suit' that started all the fuss was not her design but that of Elizabeth Smith Miller.

Both were highly active in the American women's rights movement of the 1850s; Bloomer's biweekly newspaper, *The Lily*, was a staunch advocate of the dress reform required to liberate women from the kind of cumbersome and restraining attire that prevented them from doing anything more strenuous than smiling and sipping tea. Miller came up with a well-intentioned but quite risible outfit comprising a tight-fitting jacket with Turkish-style 'harem' pants under a knee-length hooped skirt, the whole nightmare crowned by a broad-brimmed hat that left the wearer looking like a double-decker mushroom. Miller, it seems, had sufficient sense not to venture into public view wearing her own creation but not so Mrs Bloomer, whose repeated forays into society caused such howls of derision from men and women alike that she soon divested herself of her bloomers. She spent the rest of her life trying to do likewise with the link between her name and the billowing knickers, then much in vogue, that resembled the harem pants of the aforementioned fashion disaster. The outfit was such a failure that it is thought to have inspired 'bloomer' as a term for any glaring faux pas or failure.

And general usage was not yet finished with Amelia; the loaf known as a 'bloomer' likely takes its name from the fact that it is shaped like one leg of a pair of bloomers.

As things turned out, Miller was a bit before her time: the outfit, in a modified form, made a comeback in the 1890s when the cycling craze resurrected the demand for practical clothing that would let women take to the road.

BOWLER HAT and PHALLUS

The Proto-Indo-European language, or PIE for short, endured until circa 3500 BC and its root of 'bhel', to swell or blossom, produced 'bhol', a leaf or a bud, a blending of both producing the Greek 'phyllon', a leaf, which turns green and swells with the help of 'chlorophyll'. Those original PIE roots also produced terms such as 'bowl' and 'bell', so named for their shape; etymologically speaking, 'phallus' only properly applies to a penis swollen to erection by blood. 'Bole', 'bale' and 'ball' are also close cognates.

There have been several fanciful attempts to link the city hat to a Mr Bowler or, and even more fancifully, to a nebulous Frenchman called Beaulieu, but the mundane truth is that it started life as a bowl-shaped country riding hat, first made in 1849 for Edward Coke, brother of the 2nd Earl of Leicester. It became popular in London via the criminal elements, since the hat, designed as riding safety wear, could withstand a blow that would crush any other headgear. Its rigidity of structure made it, and not the Stetson, the most popular hat in the American West. Bowlers were also shipped in their thousands to South America as safety hats for the European railway construction teams, but when the gangers realised the local women would do anything to get their hands on such a hat they were traded for sexual favours, thereby starting the fashion that endures among the Bolivian Quechua women to this day.

BUCK and BUTCHER

Slight confusion here as 'buck' is today more commonly used of male deer despite its deriving from the Old English 'bucca', a male goat. The early northern French cognate of 'bouch' expanded into 'boucherie', a vendor of goat meat, whence our 'butcher'. (The strong German beer called Bock is frequently marketed with the image of such a creature, but the reason for the name is now obscure; perhaps it is simply that the beer packs a punch like a head-butt from a goat?) The 'sawbuck' is named for its projections like goats' horns and the 'bucking' of a horse resembles a leaping goat; from the incognate French 'chèvre', a goat, we get 'chevron', a shape suggestive of two goat reared up in combat. But, as seen in words such as 'springbok', by the seventeenth century the term was more commonly used of a male deer, which takes us to 'buck' as slang for 'dollar'.

The game of poker emerged in New Orleans in the early nineteenth century, as a simple variant of the game of brag; it likely took its name from the French 'poque', a bluff or boast. In some forms of the game, a player needed to have a pair of jacks or better to open the betting, hence 'jackpot'. It was also then the form to stack all discarded cards on the bottom of the deck at the end of each round and to refrain from shuffling between rounds, to allow the more astute players to figure out the odds of certain cards rising again to the top. A piece of heavy-gauge buckshot was moved round the table to mark the next dealer and a popular way of throwing a curve into the order of the cards was to miss one's turn at deal by simply 'passing the buck' onto the next player. In the eastern casinos and on the Mississippi gambling boats, a silver dollar was used to mark the dealer but it was still called the 'buck'.

Mark Twain recorded that 'passing the buck' was quite common in American slang in Virginia City in 1862, when he was working there as a reporter; it first appeared in print in the July 1865 edition of *The Weekly New Mexican*, paradoxically a monthly publication. Poker-mad President Harry S Truman was famous for having on his desk in the Oval Office a sign reading 'The Buck Stops Here'.[1]

BUCKLE and SWASHBUCKLE

Some Roman soldier's helmets (from the fourth century BC) were secured by a leather strap with a tine-and-clasp fastening on the left-hand side of his face; with 'bucca' being the Latin for 'cheek', the diminutive 'buccula' was applied to the fixing. If a wall or

---

[1] Truman's middle name was S, plain and simple, and thus needs no full stop. His parents gave him that 'name' so as not to upset either of his grandfathers, Anderson Shipp Truman and Solomon Young.

sheet of steel 'buckles', it is a reference to it starting to bell out like a cheek.

Akin to 'swish' and probably 'wash', 'swash' denoted a scything sword-swipe while 'buckler' denoted a small, convex parrying shield. 'Swash-and-buckle' denoted the kind of sword fighting in which enthusiasm and brute force replaced skill and strategy, with 'swashbuckler' emerging in the mid-1500s to denote a swaggering braggart.

The Latin 'bucca' entered Old French as 'boche', a cheek, but the later form 'bouche' shifted to the mouth. By extension, the French also used 'bouche' for a harbour; Henry VIII's celebrated 1544 capture of the Boulogne Bouche prompted the naming of countless London pubs, which in time corrupted to the Cockney favourite The Old Bull and Bush.

BUFF and BUFFALO

In the modern sense of an enthusiast, the former is derived directly from the latter, as indeed is 'in the buff', with nakedness reminiscent of the colour of undyed buffalo hide.

The soldiers of the formative United States of America valued a good buffalo coat; it not only kept them warm but was also the closest thing to body armour they had. Before there were any formalised fire brigades drawn up in the US, the duty of firefighting fell to the local militia, who also found such coats good protection against the flames they tackled. In the 1850s, regular brigades were formed and these new professionals were routinely irked by the appearance of the old irregulars, who insisted on turning out in their coats to 'help'. In nineteenth-century American firemen's slang, 'buff' spread from being specific to such men to denoting anyone who just loved to watch some poor sod's house burn down, and from 'fire buff' the term spread to the devotee of any activity, 'opera buff' and 'movie buff' being obvious examples.

BULLDOZER and BULLWHIP

The 'bullwhip' is not so named because it was used on bulls but rather because it was made *from* such creatures, with the handle often formed from what was genteelly known as the bull's pizzle.

In eighteenth-century America, 'bulldoser' described anything perceived as being able to issue a dose of force sufficient to quell a bull – heavy hammers, heavy-calibre pistols and large whips all attracted the term. In the post-bellum Southern states of 1865, those newly enfranchised African Americans brave enough to turn out to the polling stations found themselves confronted by a shoulder-to-shoulder line of Klansmen who walked forwards with whips to relentlessly drive them back. The press dubbed the KKK's tactics 'bulldosing' or 'bulldozing'.

In relation to its more modern sense of earth-moving machines, in the Southern states the term was applied to the heavy blade dragged across uneven ground by teams of horses, and later, globally, to the mechanical version. To be a trifle pedantic, 'bulldozer' only denoted the blade at the front of such machines, not the machine itself.

BUST and **BUST**

As meaning the female breast and a truncated statue, both derive from the Latin 'bustum', a tomb.

In early Rome the entrance to the crypts of the wealthy had on either side fluted columns surmounted by representations of female funeral deities, shown only from the midriff up and with breasts exposed. The sculptural use of 'bust' first emerged in the mid-to-late 1600s with the female-specific use first noted in 1819 in Byron's *Don Juan*: 'There was an Irish lady, to whose bust I ne'er saw justice done.'

The other 'bust', meaning broken, financially or otherwise, is an early-nineteenth-century American variant of 'burst'.

BUTLER and **SCUTTLEBUTT**

Both sired by the English 'butt', a cask or barrel, with the butler's prime duty once being the care and security of the wine cellar. Although now a popular name for a café or snack bar, 'buttery' has no connection to 'butter', as the term denoted the butler's storehouse, which also kept secure some of the more expensive foods of the household.

Now a Navy term for gossip, the 'scuttlebutt' was the fresh-water barrel kept on deck with a hole, or scuttle, cut through its midpoint to prevent overfilling. Naturally, when sailors gathered about it for a drink they exchanged rumours and tittle-tattle. A ship is 'scuttled' by the opening of the seacocks, and 'scuttle' is the correct term for the circular cabin window; 'porthole' described only the aperture through which cannons were fired.

BUXOM and AKIMBO

Buxom can be traced to the Old English 'bugan', to bow or bend, this producing the Middle English 'buhsum', to denote those pliant to the will of others. By the thirteenth century the modern spelling had emerged, with the term still meaning 'willing to oblige' but applicable to either sex and with no overtones of corporeal size; not until the nineteenth century did the term become restricted to women of generous physical proportions.

Given the original and proper meaning of the term, men had for centuries been only too pleased to encounter 'buxom' women, no matter their shape or size, and it doesn't take a genius to figure out in which department men wished women to be buxom. With fashion in the nineteenth century favouring women of, shall we say, corporeal amplitude, it was women of *this* shape that men desired to be buxom, so the term sidestepped from the desired disposition to the shape of the woman so disposed.

'Akimbo' is an implosion of the expression 'in kenebow', arms sharply bent or bowed, with the first syllable possibly a donation from the Icelandic 'keng', a bend, whence also 'kink' and the more modern 'kinky', denoting those of a distinct sexual bent. Others see that first element as influence from 'keen' as used to mean sharp, as in 'as keen as mustard'; opinion on the matter is divided, to say the least. Either way, although 'akimbo' properly describes the stance of clenched fists on hips, à la pantomime principal boy, it is moving inexorably towards a meaning of flung apart or splayed, through people wrongly talking of women with their legs akimbo – a position that, in the proper sense of the term, they would be hard-pushed to achieve.

CAB and CAPRICIOUS

In Latin a goat was either 'caper' (male) or 'capra' (female), with the first transferring unchanged into sixteenth-century English to denote antics and frivolities. The edible 'caper' is possibly named for the pungent flavours leaping about on the tongue like a gustatory goat, or for grazing Mediterranean goats exhibiting a preference for the plant. With much the same meaning as 'caper' in English, 'capriole' arose in French before morphing to 'cabriole', a leap or caper, which was applied to the light two-passenger carriages that sat on such high springs that they leapt at the slightest bump. Thus 'cabriolet' is a cognate of 'capricious' and the kind of light composition known as a 'capriccio'; 'cabriolet' was adopted into eighteenth-century English only to be cut down to its first syllable by early-nineteenth-century usage.

York-based architect Joseph Hansom unveiled his eponymous 'cab' in 1834, but the design now recognised as such, with the driver sitting high at the rear, resulted from a redesign by David Chapman in 1836. As for 'hackney cab', this comes from the Dutch 'hakkenij', a workaday horse, which, after a spell in French as 'haquenée', arrived as early as 1506 in English as 'hackney' – so attempts to link the origin of the term to the London Borough of Hackney are fruitless, not least because Hackney was at the time but a sleepy village. Having soon taken on the meaning of an animal rented out for work, 'hackney' or 'hack' was also applied to a common prostitute and, by extension, a drudge writer hired out on piecework.

The domestic equivalent of a hackney horse was the 'hobby horse', ridden daily over the same routes to complete the same routine tasks, hence that term as applied to a pet subject that the devotee 'rides' to death. 'Hobby' on its own, meaning an all-absorbing pastime, is not seen until the mid-1800s.

Taking name from the Latin 'tax', a charge, the first taxi meters were trialled in the last of London's horse-drawn carriages, but only came into widespread use in the horseless versions that followed – thereby allowing 'taxi' to replace both 'hansom' and 'hackney' in the early years of the twentieth century. Aeroplanes are also said to 'taxi' on the airport apron, since they look like cabs cruising for trade.

CABBAGE and BOCHE

Since the Middle Ages, the French have been using 'caboche'

for anything heavy and round, which is why that term entered English as 'cabbage'. The French also used it of the kind of heavy, dome-headed nails one sees in the construction of church and castle doors, these requiring a certain degree of brute force to be driven home, which led to the term being extended to those deemed stupid. In its truncated form, 'boche', the term was applied to the Germans throughout World War I and beyond.

Going back to those nails: to prevent the deconstruction of the door by the enemy without, the 'caboches' employed were of far greater length than was required to span the outer panel and the inner baton. This protruding extra couple of inches were hammered over and flattened against the interior of the door in a process called 'dead-nailing', hence 'as dead as a doornail'.

CALF and CAVE-IN

In the mid-eighteenth century, specialist Dutch labour was imported to drain and secure the East Anglian fens by the digging of drainage trenches and so forth. The Dutch had a word, 'uitkalven', to describe the watery gush of a calf falling from its standing mother, and the labourers, in ever-present danger of their trenches collapsing in on them, coined 'inkalven' for the watery gush that threatened to engulf them. When this, or the shorter 'kalven', was heard by the locals it was corrupted to 'cave-in', through imagery of a cave collapsing on the occupants.

The calf muscle in the human leg has a profile thought reminiscent of the belly of a pregnant cow, while glaciers 'giving birth' to icebergs are also said to 'calve'.

CANARY and CYNIC

The group of islands from which the birds hail are now under Spanish control but were first named the Canariae Insulae (Islands of the Dogs) by the Romans, for the large number of wild dogs living there. London's Canary Wharf, originally called Rum Wharf, was thus renamed in 1936 when it started to act as the receiving port for fruit from the islands. (Coincidentally, Canary Wharf is located on the Isle of Dogs.) Although 'Canary' is rare as a surname, the drunken prostitute born Martha Canary became famous in the American West as Calamity Jane, perhaps for her disastrous bedroom antics, among several unverifiable explanations (the most attractive being that she was wont to warn men that to offend her was to 'court calamity'.)

'Cynic' was first attached to a new school of philosophy founded by Antisthenes (445–365 BC), which met at a public Athenian gymnasium called the Cynosarges, or the Swift Dog, from the legend that an opportunistic dog had rushed into the temple previously located there, to grab and make off with a sacrifice being prepared for devotion to Hercules. ('Gymnasium' is based on the Greek 'gymnos', naked, as those who met in the original gymnasiums, either to train or debate, did so in the buff.) The Cynics rose to prominence under Diogenes, their name cemented by the fact that he was generally known as The Dog for his lack of attention to personal hygiene. The Cynics' tendency to doubt or dismiss all previous teachings led the term to where it stands today.

Although 'dog days' can denote any heatwave, properly this

33

is the period from 24 July to 24 August, when Greeks and Romans noticed that Sirius, otherwise known as the Dog Star for its prominence in the constellation of Canis Major, was particularly prominent; they presumed its increased visibility was responsible for the temperatures during that spell. Also allied is 'cynosure', the focus of all attention. Before Ursa Minor, or the Little Bear, was so named, it was thought to resemble a small dog, with the Pole Star, so crucial to navigation, called Cynosura, or the Dog's Tail.

CANNIBAL and CARIBBEAN

When Columbus crossed the Atlantic he thought himself bound for India, so when he arrived at some islands he called them the West Indies and immediately set about enslaving the locals on the spurious grounds that they were man-eaters, and thus beyond the protection of God. The peoples enslaved called themselves the Caniba, a name from which Columbus constructed 'cannibal', and with the letters N, R and L being interchangeable in the native language, he opted for 'Caribbean' for the location to avoid confusion and the frightening-off of potential settlers.

CARNIVAL and CARNATION

Although the word is now more commonly associated with the frivolities of Notting Hill and Rio, 'Carnival' was more properly the Christian festival that preceded Lent. Lent was of course a fasting period so 'Carnival' derives from the Latin 'carne', flesh or meat, and 'levare', to remove or put away. Because of this, certain perishables had to be used up, hence Shrovetide pancakes, the day being named from 'shrift', a confession. Those given 'short shrift' were criminals on the gallows who, not given sufficient time to make their peace with their maker, were dropped hurriedly and out of hand.

The 'carnation' is named for the flesh-like colour of its petals, with 'carnivore', 'carnal', 'incarnation' and 'charnel' obvious cognates.

CASTLE and CASTRATE

The Latin 'castus' means 'to cut off' or 'separate' and, by extension, also means 'pure'. The 'caste' system in India separates the various strata of society and the 'cast' of a play are separate from the production and behind-the-scenes people. Those kept away from sexual activity are 'chaste', with sexual activity deemed impure being termed 'incastus' or 'incest'; transgressors are made pure again by 'chastisement' or 'castigation'.

'Castle' derives from the Latin 'castra', a place cut off or marked as separate for the purposes of a military encampment, this sense continuing to the stone-built fortification that was cut off from its surroundings by its walls. Although 'caster', 'chester' and 'cester' at the end of a town's name frequently do indicate the one-time presence of a Roman fort, the rule is by no means firm, as the suffixes can equally indicate the location of a pre-Roman fortification or one where the Romans built nothing at all. The Spanish name 'Castro' is also from the same source. This sense of 'cut off' is also clear in French with the link between 'château' and 'couteau', a knife; the housekeeper of a château was the chatelain, a term now applied to a bunch of keys or trinkets worn on a chain about the waist.

As for 'castrate', the link is painfully clear, but contrary to popular usage the term refers to the excision of the testes only; the suitably named Lorena Bobbitt did not 'castrate' her husband – she merely cut off his penis and tossed it out of the car window – but it is doubtful whether he gleaned any comfort from this exercise in semantics. To its shame the Vatican for centuries persistently castrated choirboys so they could continue singing in high register; perhaps they should have read their own Bible, as Deuteronomy 23:1 clearly states that anyone whose testes are crushed or excised is excluded from the assembly of the Lord. Alessandro Moreschi, the last of the Sistine Castrati, died as recently as 1922.

CHAPEL and SCAPEGOAT

Still much venerated in France, St Martin of Tours (d. AD 397) was a Roman soldier who, on seeing a shivering beggar at the gates of Amiens, is said to have divided his centurion's cloak in two and shared it with the unfortunate. He went on his way, only to be later confronted by Jesus holding the other half of the cloak and telling him to quit the army and put himself under the control of the Bishop of Poitiers. Frankish and early French kings never went on campaign without St Martin's cape, or 'chape', in a reliquary; at various points on the journey, one man would be told to leave the army and build a small 'chapel' to St

Martin and then to remain there as custodian, or 'chaplain'. Also cognate is the name of the 'Capuchin' monks, identified by their distinctive hooded cloaks, hence also the 'capuchin monkey' with its cowl of hair ('monkey' itself means 'little monk'); cappuccino coffee, with its cowl-shaped topping of whipped cream, is in fact so named because its colour resembles the garments worn by Capuchin monks.

Building on the Early French 'eschaper' and the Early Italian 'scappare', both meaning 'to slip out of the cape', early fourteenth-century English created 'escape' to describe a sword-fighting manoeuvre common to the era. Opponents would try to grab the opponent's cape and tug it about to gain advantage, leaving the wearer no option but to untie the cladding at the neck and, quite literally, slip out of the cape and make off. The Italian version of the term is also the likely progenitor of 'scarper'.

On the Day of Atonement ('at one' with God) in the early Hebrew culture, two goats were selected at random for a ritual during which one was dedicated to Azazel, the fallen angel, while the other was sacrificed on the altar. The collective transgressions of the congregation were then laid on the head of the remaining goat, which was returned to the wilderness so that it could make off with its burden of sins. In English versions of the Bible, the Azazel-goat, who unlike his modern namesake seems to have got the best of the deal, was referred to as the 'escapegoat' before the 'e' was abandoned in the early 1500s to leave 'scapegoat'; it was not until the mid-1800s that the term was applied in metaphor to people.

CARBINE and SCARAB

From the establishment of the Roman Empire in 27 BC – Julius Caesar was thus never Emperor as he died in 44 BC – and throughout medieval Italy, it fell to the slaves of Rome to haul away plague victims for burial beyond the city walls. This earned the slaves the nickname of 'scarabini', an allusion to the scarab beetle, which is infamous for rolling away its own unpleasant cargo. In the seventeenth century, the Savoyard states of pre-unification Italy hired mercenary brigades of light mounted skirmishers who, during the recurrent bouts of plague, were saddled with both the burial duties and the old nickname.

These more modern scarabini found the long musket of the day far too unwieldy to be used on horseback so they favoured a shortened version, which also acquired the nickname before losing the 's' to become 'carabiniere', which, by 1640, had appeared in English as 'carbine'. After the unification of Italy in 1861, these units were incorporated into the new national army, and although tourists wrongly presume the present-day Italian 'Carabinieri' to be civil police, they are in fact military personnel, as indeed were the French gendarmes ('armed men') until they were recently transferred to the control of the Ministry of the Interior.

CATAPULT and CATASTROPHE

Both words are rooted in Greek, with the first based on 'kata', down, and 'pallein', to hurl, as it was the first device designed to rain rocks down on the heads of the enemy. In the form of 'katastrophe', a turning down, the second term originally denoted the final act of a Greek play and only came to its present meaning because of the way such plays tended to end with one half of the cast stabbing the other.

Through the common 'cata-' element, meaning 'down', both terms are cognates of the underground 'catacomb', the 'catatonic' state in which the bodily functions are all toned down, 'cataract' and 'cataclysm', both of which originally denoted a strong waterfall or deluge. Also allied are the 'catarrh' that runs down the nose, the 'catalytic' converter that breaks things down into their various 'categories', the 'catheter' that allows a downflow, the 'catalogue' that lists down items and the 'cathedral', which houses the local bishop's throne, or 'cathedra', on which he sits down to make pronouncements on matters of faith, hence speaking 'ex cathedra'.

CHAMPAGNE and SCAMP

Both derive from the French 'champ', a field.

Now a protected French product, the fizzy wine marked 'Champagne' comes from the region of the same name, which is noted for its rolling fields. It should be pointed out, however, that Champagne was first made by the English: Christopher Merret was knocking out bubbly in Gloucester in 1662, nearly thirty years before the upstart Dom Pérignon muscled in on the game.

But no matter; although now restricted to endearingly naughty children, the 'scamp' was originally a despised figure who joined an army for the food and shelter but decamped, or 'escamped', the night before the battle. Allied terms are the 'champignons' harvested from the fields, the university 'campus' and, of course, the 'champion' who took the field, sweeping all before him.

CHANCELLOR and CANCEL

Those with business in a Roman court of law had to first wait their turn in the lobia, an external porch covered with leafy vines for shade. This entered English as 'lobby', with terms such as 'lobate', leaf-like, a close relative. When summoned, the petitioner had to present the facts of his case to one of the 'cancellarii', the court ushers so named because they always sat behind 'cancelli', or lattice-work screens and any cheque or document that is 'cancelled' is defaced with a hatchwork of lines indicating annulment.

The office of the cancellarii grew to such importance in Rome that the term was later adopted by many countries with the Court of 'Chancery', under the auspices of the 'Chancellor' of the Exchequer, becoming so well known for the protracted complexity of its deliberations that it formed the nub of the plot of Dickens' *Bleak House*, in which many of the protagonists' lives are locked in limbo pending the outcome of Jarndyce v. Jarndyce, a case under Chancery. The wrestling hold called 'chancery', in which one party's head is held in a lock by the other, is likewise named for the difficulty of extricating oneself from such an undignified predicament.

CHRONIC and CRONY

Based on the Greek 'khronos', time, 'chronic' is today much misused as a synonym for 'terrible' or 'lamentable' through a misunderstanding of the term's medical use. A 'chronic condition' may or may not be chronic in the misused sense; the term simply denotes conditions that are enduring instead of those of sudden onset, which are acute. Enduring happiness could legitimately be described as chronic.

As for 'crony', this started life as seventeenth-century university slang, probably at Cambridge, for a friend who was up at the same time, and 'chronometer' and 'synchronise' are obvious cognates as indeed is the 'chronicle' that lists events in time-order.

Another example of time-related university slang is 'tandem', which is the Latin for 'at length', but only in the sense of time, not physical measurement. In Oxbridge slang this was humorously ascribed in the mid-1780s to a carriage drawn by two horses, one behind the other, and, a hundred years later, to the two-seater bicycle carrying the riders in a similar formation. Failing to see the linguistic pun, non-university people picked up the term in the sense of 'two' or 'together', and were soon talking of events occurring 'in tandem' which, etymologically speaking, makes no sense whatsoever.

CHUM and CHAMBERLAIN

The Latin 'camera', a vaulted chamber, was adopted by English to form 'chamber' and 'camber', this second term born of the vaulted aspect of the Latin 'camera'. Those who bunked together enjoyed 'camaraderie', with university slang corrupting 'chamber-mate' into 'chumber-mate', whence 'chum'. The allied 'comrade' is now only really heard in military circles or communist ones. The Italian, Mafia-style 'Camorra' took its name from the organisation's secret meetings being held 'in camera', in closed rooms.

The now-elite position of 'Chamberlain' began life as the bedchamber flunky to the king, his main duty being to stand attendance in the royal privy. As the office of Chamberlain grew in importance, the humiliating task of inter-gluteal burnishing, shall we say, was passed on to the Groom of the Stool, an office that survived until it was finally and mercifully abolished by Edward VII. Either way, the intimacy of the relationship between the royal and his Chamberlain ensured a swift rise in the household.

The modern 'camera' is so named for the picture, in the early models at least, being captured on film on the little 'room' inside the box.

CIAO and SLAVE

In the Early Middle Ages, German slavers forced so many Slavs into servitude that 'Slav(e)' itself became the accepted term for someone in such bondage. From the Middle Latin 'sclavus', Slav or slave, early Italian built 'schiavo', which now presents as 'ciao' – the shout of 'schiavo!' was used to both summon and dismiss a slave, which perhaps explains why in modern Italian the term can mean both 'hello' and 'goodbye'.

In Medieval England a summoned slave would reply, 'Anon!',

meaning 'in one', or 'at once'; how the term acquired overtones of 'in my own sweet time' is anybody's guess, for no summoned slave would reply with a term informing his master that he would comply when he was good and ready.

Interestingly enough, the Czech for a slave is 'robotnik', a term introduced to English through the tremendous popularity of the sci-fi play *Rossum's Universal Robots* (1920) by the Czech playwright Karel Čapek, which took London by storm.

CLEAVE and CLEVER

'Cleave' seems to present the puzzlement of being its own antonym, in that the term can denote sticking together or splitting asunder. Middle English had two separate terms, 'cleofian', to glue or stick together, and 'cleofan', the progenitor of 'cleaver' and 'cloven', which meant 'to split apart'. People just got bored of the differentiating 'I' and took to spelling both the same; it was left to context to guide the reader.

Centuries ago, 'clivers' described the talons of a bird of prey that could split the prey in half, and 'clever' first described people who were tenacious, adroit and perhaps a tad cunning; not until the mid-nineteenth century did the term start to be used of mental capacity.

CLIMATE and CLIMAX

The Greek 'klima', to slope, exposes the popular misuse of 'climax' to denote a high point or culmination, usage dismissed by the *OED* somewhat loftily as being 'due to popular ignorance'.

Properly the term denotes an ascending scale, so 'climate' refers to the weather patterns observed in the distance where the sky seems to 'klima' down to meet the horizon. The cognate 'klinein' produced terms such as 'incline' and the 'clinic' in which patients 'recline' on a bed awaiting medical attention.

Although not in any way etymologically linked, similar misunderstanding attaches to 'crescendo', as derived from the Latin 'crescere', to grow. As does 'climax', 'crescendo' properly describes an ascending scale and not a cacophonic finale; a 'crescent' moon is one starting to grow back to full orb, but after the symbol was adopted by twelfth-century Muslim nations to indicate their growing power, Westerners started to use 'crescent' to denote shape rather than any indication of waxing.

The supposedly French 'croissant' is in fact a Viennese plagiarism of the Hungarian 'kifli', alleged first baked in 1686 to celebrate the lifting of the Ottoman siege of Buda, the town that, in 1873, would join with its old rival, Pest, on the opposite bank of the Danube, to become Budapest. Either way, if the tale is true, the pastries were baked in the shape of the Muslim symbol newly banished from their walls.

CLIQUE and CLICHÉ

Paris in the 1820s saw the rise of a body of professional theatregoers who, paid to attend, would cry, howl with laughter, or give up thunderous applause at the right moment. The less worthy the play the more it was in need of such professional 'clappers', hence 'clap-trap'. Called the 'claque' for the noise they generated, these people were not held in very high esteem, even by those who depended on them for a good opening night, so they formed their own little society, or 'clique', on the fringes of the theatrical world.

As for the 'cliché', this was the printing plate that 'clicked' or 'claqued' up and down as it relentlessly churned out the same text following the 1720 advent of stereotype printing, the name of that very process having become, in general speech at least, a synonym for 'cliché'.

COACH and COACH

As denoting a tutor and a means of transport, both are linked to the Hungarian town of Kocs.

The fifteenth-century Hungarian army was the first to realise that the fresher men felt when they got to battle, the better they would perform against an enemy who had perhaps been marching for weeks. To this end the Hungarian infantry was transported on wagons with bench seating that were mass-produced in Kocs, near Budapest. After the fourteenth-century wars with the Ottomans these 'kocszekkers', as they were known, were hived off for public transport, and by the time the vehicles had arrived in England, this name had, perhaps mercifully, been truncated to 'kocs', which is pronounced something akin to 'kotch'.

It was nineteenth-century university slang that appropriated 'coach' as a nickname for a specialised tutor who 'transported' the student swiftly to his sporting or academic 'destination'.

COCKPIT and COCKTAIL

In the wooden warships of old, the space below the lower gun deck served as the midshipmen's mess, but in times of battle this was commandeered by the ship's surgeon to do the best he could with the horrendous injuries caused by grapeshot or wooden splinters the size of javelins. It was this use that earned the area the nickname 'the cockpit' for all its blood and gore, a reference to the arena where such birds would fight to the death. With the advent of smaller ships – yachts and the like – the term transferred to the corresponding area, which housed the steering wheel and navigational aids, and from this it was but a short step to the flight deck of a modern plane.

There is no shortage of outlandish theories purporting to be the true origin of 'cocktail', which in fact was born in the horse-racing fraternity. Unlike racing stock, which had their bloodlines meticulously recorded, everyday working animals were of unknown lineage. Generally they had their tails cut short for the sake of cleanliness, this causing the tail to stand 'cocked' up through lack of weight. In racing circles, 'cock tail' was used of a horse with racing ability but whose bloodline was uncertain, and the term seems to have shifted to drinks of equally uncertain ingredients in the early part of the nineteenth century. In relation to mixed drinks, the term is first noted in the 1806 American publication *Balance and Columbian Repository*, in which 'cock tail' is the presented form. In America, such a horse was also known as a 'bang tail' and the more symmetrically severe of women's hairstyles are still called 'bangs'.

A close cousin of both terms is 'cockney', which started life in the Middle Ages as 'coken-ey', a cock's egg, a biological impossibility that in rural England described the kind of yolkless egg laid by a young hen. Since such eggs were worthless, the term was applied to simpletons, layabouts and townies who, ignorant of country ways, always seemed to be lost and out of place in such regions. Not until the seventeenth century did the term become London-specific, and it was later still before it was restricted to those born within earshot of the bells of St Mary-le-Bow Church in the Cheapside district.

CODSWALLOP and CODPIECE

His surname indicating he came from a family of purse-makers, Hiram Codd filed a patent for an airtight bottle for fizzy drinks in 1872. Still used in Japan as a marketing gimmick by the makers of the ever-popular drink Ramune, the design incorporated a glass ball in the neck that was held tight against a rubber washer by the pressure generated by the effervescence of the contents. 'Wallop' has long served in English as slang for beer and it was the drinking fraternity's scorn for lemonade that produced 'cod(d)swallop' for something of little or no worth.

The Old and Middle English 'codd', 'codde' or 'cod' all meant a small bag or pouch, with the fish gaining its name for its sack-like profile, but the term could also denote the scrotum, otherwise known as the 'balzac' (or 'ball-sack'), which oddly enough was the surname of the celebrated French writer. Reaching the peak of its popularity in the mid-1500s, the 'codpiece' was a reinforced genital bracket worn by men to protrude from their hose in a grotesque manner, sometimes with a snarling face on the tip of the exaggerated penile projection, just to make the point; (all mouth and trousers, which brings to mind M Balzac's novel, *Illusions Perdues*.) A bizarre trend to say the least, these mercifully faded from use in the 1590s.

COMEDY and TRAGEDY

Although now at opposite ends of the theatrical spectrum, both are united by the Greek 'oide' (ode), a song or story.

Neither the Greek 'komoidia' nor the Roman 'comoedicus' were intended to elicit belly laughs; the terms instead denoted any tale with a happy ending or at least one that did not end in the wholesale slaughter of the cast. This meaning was still prominent when Dante wrote his *Divine Comedy*, completed in 1320. As for the 'tragedy' so dear to the Greek theatrical heart, this is derived from 'tragos', goat, and 'oide', as it was once the custom to award a goat as a prize to the teller of the most depressing tale of the night.

CONSTABLE and STABLE

With horsepower essential to everyday life, agriculture and war, the breeding of horses was serious business throughout most of history, with the officer in charge of such production accorded the title count of the stables, shortened to 'constable'. Under the constable was the mareschal, the man responsible for sourcing the brood mares, whose title evolved into 'marshal', whence the military rank of field marshal. One such breeding unit of industrial size was set up by Otto the Great, circa AD 950, on the edge of Germany's Black Forest, and the town that grew up around it, Stuttgart, or Stud Farm, still has a prancing horse as its coat of arms, later adopted by Porsche, whose cars were first manufactured in that city

It is also worth mentioning that as the emphasis shifted from pigs to cattle, the redundant styward was found other duties in the household, with his title altering to 'steward'.

CRETIN and CHRISTIAN

Both derive from the Greek 'christos', anointed, with the name Christ meaning 'the anointed one'. The link is perhaps clearer in the French for 'Christian', which was and is 'Chrétien'.

'Cretinism' is a condition caused by thyroid malfunction due to lack of iodine; the endemic form was in medieval times centred in Switzerland and the Pyrenees, where the soil was notoriously iodine-deficient. 'Cretins' were easily identifiable by their mental impairment, stunted growth and the presentation of goitres, which the Church claimed made them blessed in their innocence, through having been touched by the hand of God in the womb. The simple are still said to be 'a bit touched'.

In Heaven, as on earth, there is a pecking order, and while cretins and their like could be blamed neither for their condition nor their inability to accept the word of God, it simply would not have been on to have them drooling all over Heaven proper. Conversely it would have seemed harsh to consign them to Hell or even to Limbo, where the souls of those born before the coming of Christ had to wait 'in Limbo' for the Final Judgement. So the Church invented the segregated Fools' Paradise, an expression still synonymous with 'Cloud Cuckoo Land'.

CROUP and CROUPIER

Both take their origins directly from the Middle French 'croupe', a horse's arse.

Knights of the time preferred to travel fast and light, taking along but the one servant who rode pillion, behind the saddle, on the horse's rump. When camped together or upon meeting at inns, gambling was the norm for such men, with one of their 'croupiers' nominated the dealer or handler of the die for the night, to prevent any unseemly accusations of cheating. As for 'croup', the noisy cough, this was thought reminiscent of the kind of noises one tends to hear emanating from a horse's arse.

DANDELION and INDENTURED

Teeth are the root here, with the plant taking its name from the French 'dent de lion', lion's tooth, a reference to the colour and shape of the petals.

In earlier England, a contract between two parties, such as that outlining 'indentured' labour, would be written out in duplicate on a large parchment that was then roughly torn or cut in two, with each party retaining their respective half. No two paper tears are the same and this method was intended to prevent any later substitution of altered text, by either party, as the two original halves could always be detected by the marrying up of the 'toothed' edges.

Some legal documents still present a 'toothed' border as a nod to this now-lapsed tradition, but documents relating to the binding of a single party to an agreement, such as a person changing their name, are always presented on paper with clean-cut, or polled, edges, hence 'deed poll'.

DASHBOARD and SLAPDASH

Several terms transferred from the horse-drawn carriage to the horseless variety; coaches used to have a heavy storage box, or 'boîte', as it was in French, strapped to the rear for storage, hence the car 'boot' (or 'trunk', as it is in America). As for 'dashboard', this first described the broad plank angled in front of coach drivers to protect them from mud 'dashed' up by the horses. The ultimate root is the Swedish 'daska', to beat, strike or move quickly, so you can as easily dash off a letter as you can see your hopes dashed.

The echoic German 'schlappe', a blow with the open hand, was added to 'dash' to describe the kind of coarse plastering applied to wall with no attempt at effecting a smooth finish.

DEADLINE and LINGERIE

Lingerie is named from the French 'linge', a linen garment, with 'linen' itself a reference to the straight and linear weave so typical of such fabric. 'Deadline' is of more martial origins.

During the American Civil War the largest camp for the containment of Union POWs was established at Andersonville in Georgia, and run on a harsh regime that was not designed to be relished. Running parallel to the main stockade wall was a white line, and any prisoner stepping over that line was presumed to be attempting escape and shot out of hand. In the post-war trial of the camp's commanding officer, Henry Wirz, the press made so much of this 'deadline', as they christened it, that it was already in general use by the time Wirz was shot.

DECIMATE and DECEMBER

Although the former is now used to denote wholesale slaughter, this is not its proper meaning. As the first element of the term indicates, it means to kill only one tenth. 'Decimation' was a punishment inflicted in Ancient Rome, either on its own troops in the event of mutiny or cowardice, or on the survivors of vanquished armies that had employed dirty tactics or failed to fight with courage. As a punishment it lapsed for a while but was reinstated by Crassus during his hunt for Spartacus in 71 BC.

'December' presents an apparent anomaly as it is our twelfth rather than tenth month, but in the Roman calendar it was the tenth month of a year that began in March. This shift is also seen in September, October and November, whose names indicate 'seven', 'eight' and 'nine', despite their being our ninth, tenth and eleventh months of the year.

DELPHINIUM and DAUPHIN

Both of these come from the Latin 'delphos', womb. In the case of the flower, it was fancied that its nectary resembled the shape of said organ, while the dolphin, initially thought to be a fish, was likewise named for inexplicably possessing such an organ.

As for the 'dauphin', he took his title from the ancient

principality of the Dauphiné, located in the south of what is now France. Now best known for its potatoes 'dauphinoise', the area was ruled in the twelfth century by Guigues of Albon, nicknamed 'Le Dauphin' for such a creature appearing on his device. When the principality was brought under French control in the fourteenth century, one of the conditions was that the heir apparent to the French throne would always be the titular ruler of the area – so it was, if you like, a deal similar to that which produced the title of The Prince of Wales.

The London district of Adelphi was named for its architectural plans being drawn up by the Adams brothers, with the root being the Greek 'adelphos', brother, but literally 'from the same womb'. Much maligned by W. C. Fields, one of its most famous sons, Philadelphia (the City of Brotherly Love) was so named by founder William Penn, the Quaker, whose egalitarian principles set the grid pattern for subsequent American cities. Determined that no settler should have more land than any other, he laid out the parcels in equal squares. It is, incidentally, a myth that Fields's gravestone reads 'On the whole, I'd rather be in Philadelphia'; it just presents his name and dates.

Also linked is the ancient site of Delphi, where the Pythian sibyl sat guarding a pit thought to be the womb of the earth. Although separate, it is worth mention that the Latin for a womb, 'hustera', produced 'hysteria', as only women were thought capable of irrational behaviour.

DICKER and DIXIE

Bartering remained a common form of doing business for years after coins were in broad circulation – mainly because, with good reason, not everybody trusted the coins, as adulteration with base metals was a popular scam of dodgy monarchs. Indeed, many evolving currencies took their name from old bartering units such as the drachma as derived from the Greek bartering unit of a 'drakhme', a handful, but specifically a handful of arrows or obeloi. But it was still easy to get cheated, which is why 'barter', cognate of the Irish 'brath', treachery, itself meant 'to cheat or defraud'. In commercial barter, a lot of ten, or decuria, from the Latin 'decem', ten, was a standard unit, and the more decuria at stake the more the 'dickering' over the deal.

To settle disputes over the respective worth of the parcels of goods being exchanged, as well as how much might have be added to one party's goods to impose equality on the lots, an umpire was appointed to preside over a complicated ritual in which both parties put a number of coins into the judge's hat before engaging in what can only be described as a game of spoof. At various junctures in the haggle the two parties were invited to dip into the cap and then show if they were holding coins or not. Only when both men opened their hands to show they had taken more than a single coin from the hat was the deal closed; the umpire kept all the coins for his trouble. From this game of hand-in-cap we derive 'handicap', which moved to its present meaning when the horse-racing fraternity adopted the ritual to decide how much extra weight a horse might have to carry to make for a fair (or closer) race. It was from this usage that 'handicap' acquired its meaning of an impediment or an impairment.

Although it is easy to presume Dixie to be so named for its lying to the south of the Mason-Dixon Line, that line was drawn back in the 1760s and a hundred years is too long for a term to lie fallow and undetected. Again, it is dodgy currency at the root of the term, in that the Southern states of the 1830s were flooded with counterfeit notes or those issued by wildcat banks without the funds to back the paper's supposed worth. In an effort to stem the fast-ebbing trust in banknotes, the Citizens' Bank and Trust Company of New Orleans began production of highly complex notes that were printed in a mixture of French and English on a distinctive long-staple paper imported from Europe. The first notes produced were $10 bills for business circles, these having the French DIX, ten, printed on the reverse and, overnight, New Orleans became known as Dixie-Town. As these notes spread across what would become the Confederacy in 1861, by the 1850s that entire region was being called Dixie.

DISASTER and STERLING

With the economy never out of the news these days, the two terms often go hand in hand – and rightly so as both derive from the Greek 'aster', star, hence also the name of the star-shaped flower and the asterisk, which presents in stellar form. The prophets of old claimed to be able to read what was written in the stars, with those ignoring the omens doubtless bound for 'dis-aster'.

The UK currency takes its name from the Middle English 'sterre', star, and its diminutive 'sterling', little star, a device once present on medieval pennies. Taking the form of a simple indented cross, this was imposed so the coins could be broken up into fourthings, or farthings, for small change. From a one-pound block of silver the early mint could strike 240 small pennies, hence the pre-decimal UK currency structure being dictated by a pound of sterlings, which became the 'pound sterling'.

With the worth of a coin intrinsic in its gold or silver, the ungodly were not averse to clipping a bit from each coin that passed through their grasping hands, but much of this practice was halted by the addition of milling round the edge of coins, which made trimming impossible to miss. Before that addition to the minting process, all money had to be weighed out – the £ symbol but a fancy L as in 'libra', a set of scales – and from the Latin 'pendo', I weigh, we derive 'pension', 'stipend', 'expend' and 'spend'.

DOLLAR and THALIDOMIDE

Sometime around 1520, Bohemia began striking coins from silver mined in Joachimsthal, or Jacob's Valley, and such was the trust in these coins that 'joachimsthalers' gained wide currency. Naturally, such a clumsy name was not long in circulation before it was truncated to 'thaler', with the Dutch changing this to 'daler', as that was their word for 'valley'. Coins referred to as 'thalers' and 'dalers' were circulating in England and Scotland by the 1560s, with 'dolor' first noted in 1588 and 'dollar' having emerged by 1706 – so 'dollars' were in common European circulation long before settlers took them to the New World.

Until 1792, dollars in America circulated alongside the Spanish piece-of-eight, so named due to the coins having deep lines to make it easy for people to snap them into smaller pieces for change – the Americans still talk about 'two bits', 'four bits', and so on. When the dollar was adopted as the formal currency in 1792, the coins showed on their reverse an old-style 8 – a bit like an S with a line through it – to let people know they held the same value as the Spanish coins they had been used to; this symbol soon morphed into $.

Thus it is clear that 'dollar' is related to terms such as 'Neanderthal', the Neander Valley in Germany where such humanoid remains were first found, but it is also sister to darker terms such as 'thallium' and 'Thalidomide'. Colourless, tasteless, odourless and highly unlikely to be spotted by your average GP, thallium has long been known as 'the poisoner's poison'; it shows a green spike in spectroscopy and thus earns its name from the Greek 'thallia', green and luxuriant as a valley. As for Thalidomide, this was first marketed by the German company Grunenthal, a corporate name meaning, somewhat ironically, a green and pleasant valley, with the last element of the company name used as the foundation of the trade name of the horror-drug it unleashed.

DOMINOES and DAMSEL

The common root here is the Latin 'dominus', the master or lord who 'dominated' all within his 'domain' or his 'domestic' arrangements. On the continent, this produced the titles 'Dom' and 'Don', along with the feminine parallels 'Domina', 'Donna' or 'Madonna', this latter often contracted into 'Mona', as in *Mona Lisa*. The daughter of the 'madam' acquired the title 'damsel', which survives in contemporary French as 'mademoiselle'.

As for the game tiles, these took their name from the 'domino' – a word that uses 'lord' as in 'Lord God Almighty' – which was a style of French monks' hood that incorporated a black veil with two holes cut for the eyes. The name of the hood shifted to the black gaming tiles with the white spots fancied to resemble eyes peering through the ecclesiastical domino; the game was subsequently introduced to the UK by French POWs of the Napoleonic Wars. A player unable to take his turn had to indicate this temporary defeat to the other players by knocking under the table, or 'knuckling under', and as the winning side deducted from the opposition's running total the number of spots on the tiles unplayed in their hands, they were said to be 'knocking the spots off' them.

DRAG and DRAWING ROOM

'Draw', 'draft', 'draught' and 'drag' all descend from the Middle English 'drawen' and its previous presentation of 'drahen' and the Old English 'dragen', both meaning to drag or draw.

The 'draughtsman' draws lines; 'draught' beer is drawn from the barrel and the banker's 'draft' or 'draught' draws funds from an account; the game of 'draughts' requires players to withdraw pieces from the board. Fashionable residences of old always had a private room to which the men of the house could withdraw, that 'withdrawing room' now presenting as the 'drawing room'. 'Dredge' is a distant cousin and those who look like they have been dragged through a hedge backwards are 'bedraggled'.

'Drag' first arose in theatrical jargon of the mid-1800s, when the fashion of the day was floor-length skirts or dresses that dragged across the stage as the male actor, unused to such hindrance to movement, walked about the stage. 'Drag queen' is not noted prior to 1941 and such acts not welcomed into mainstream entertainment until the 1960s.

DUMB-BELL and THIMBLE

'Dumb-bell' emerged in the late seventeenth century, when archers could improve their upper-body strength by tolling the ropes on local church bells from which the clappers had been removed to ensure peace and quiet for others. The term could equally apply to the heavy handheld brass bells used to train up would-be campanologists; these too had their clappers removed as they were only for teaching the order of the chimes, as well as for exercise, which is getting closer to the modern application.

As for 'thimble', this is basically a thinning of 'thumb-bell', with 'thumb' itself tracing back to the Sanskrit 'tumbas', a kind of large cucumber, a term that entered Greek as 'tumbos' to denote the kind of elongated burial mounds that were then the fashion; 'tomb' is an obvious descendant. Acquiring overtones of thickening or swelling, 'tumbos' produced 'thumb', 'thigh', 'tumour' 'and 'tuber'. Early French adopted the term in the form of 'tufler', then 'trufler', which not only produced the swollen 'truffle' but also gave its name to inflated buffoonery – a 'trufler' was an overblown mockery that developed into the English 'trifle', first descriptive of any meaningless jest or frolic, then applied to items of no value or to frivolities, such as the dessert of same name.

E

EGYPT and GYPSY

Properly called the Rom or the Roma, the people called 'Gypsies' were originally a low-caste community who quit northern India at the opening of the eleventh century and drifted west in search of a better life. As they then moved north from Africa, the Rom travelled through Spain and into southern France, where they were thought to be Egyptians and so called the 'Egyptano', shortened to 'Gitano'. The English made the same mistake, called them 'Egyptians', which shortened to 'Gyptians' and finally to 'Gypsies'. Others trekked relentlessly across Europe, though Bohemia and into France, hence 'bohemian' for an unorthodox lifestyle.

'Gyp', to cheat or defraud, is a simple truncation of 'gypsy', and their Hindi-based language has brought many a term into

English slang. 'Kushti', good or pleasurable, produced 'cushy'; 'chavvi', an unruly child, produced 'shaver' and doubtless 'chav'; 'loke', a man, produced 'bloke'; 'pal' was Roma for a brother or friend; 'vonga', money, produced 'wonga'; and 'posh' – nothing to do with 'Port Out, Starboard Home' – was another Roma term for money or wealth, so there is, by coincidence only, a connection between 'posh' and India.

ESKIMO and HUSKY

Deriving from the old Cree Indian insult of 'askimowew', which translates as 'he eats it raw', 'Eskimo' is now considered non-PC, especially among the Arctic-dwellers themselves, who prefer to be known as the Inuit, or the People. The original Cree term was picked up by early French explorers of the frozen wastes as 'Esquimaux', which entered sixteenth-century English as 'Esquimo' before altering to the common form. The so-called 'Eskimo kiss' is not in fact a rubbing of noses but an exchange of exhaled breath, while the greatest lexicographical myth attached to these people is that they have fifty or so different words for snow; they don't.

As did their Siberian forebears who wandered across the long-lost land bridge between Russia and America, the Inuit use a breed of stout draught dog which was first called an 'Eskie', then a 'huski', this altering to 'husky' by the mid-nineteenth century.

The Siberian tribesmen from whom the Inuit are descended do not take kindly to being called Samoyed, as this is the Russian for 'self-eaters', or cannibals, instead preferring Nenets, the

People; the first element of 'Samoyed' is seen in the name of the increasingly trendy samovar, or self-boiler.

ETIQUETTE and STIGMA

In the days before glues were available, items were attached to one another by tiny wooden pins that looked like cocktail sticks, so the wooden 'stick' is the same as the 'stick' relating to glue. Pointed sticks, hot from the fire, were used to brand the guilty with a 'stigma', or mark of shame, and those with 'astigmatism' are unable to focus the eyes on a specific point. Such brands 'distinguished' – yet another cognate of both 'stick' and 'stigma' – animals and people as being apart from the common herd.

'Etiquette' began life in Middle French as 'estiquet', which detailed the billeting arrangements and was posted on a stake in front of the barracks. It entered English in the mid-1700s to denote the page that was glued into the front of a handbook given to all attending the royal court, informing them of the dos and don'ts of the day and listing who had rank above whom. 'That's the ticket', meaning 'the right thing', is a spin-off from 'etiquette'. Although incognate, 'etiquette' is reflected in 'protocol', which, basically meaning 'the first glued', denoted a similar sheet glued into the front of handbooks in diplomatic circles.

The cognate 'style' first denoted a small pointed stick used for writing, and with calligraphy styles being unique, the term shifted to refer to fashion or individual style. The 'stylus' on the resurgent gramophone is but a little stick, as is the 'stiletto', be it knife or shoe heel. Although distant cousins that have lost their initial S, the 'tiger' flies at its prey like an arrow, which was once but a pointed stick, and the 'Tigris' is a fast-flowing river.

EXCHEQUER and CHESS

The office of the 'exchequer' was created in the early fourteenth century and took its name from the Anglo-French 'escheker', chessboard, in reference to the checked cloth then used as a calculating device; the country seat of the Chancellor of the Exchequer is still called Chequers.

These, and a host of other terms, can all be traced back to 'check', as in 'to stop' – 'body check', 'checkpoint', the bank 'check' or 'cheque' that puts a stop to the availability to you of the stated amount; 'rain check' derives from rained-off American sporting events and the undated replacement tickets issued to grant admittance whenever the game was rescheduled. You have to hold yourself 'in check' if in a temper, halt an investigation while certain facts are 'checked', you 'check out' of a hotel and the game of 'checkers' involves blocking or stopping the opponent's pieces.

The cognate Old French 'echecs', softened to 'eches', entered English as 'chess', a game which comes to a sudden stop with the call of 'checkmate' the second element of that term being taken from the Old Persian call of 'shah mat', meaning 'the king is dead'.

EXPLODE and APPLAUD

Early Greek and Roman audiences did not often clap as we do, but rather they indicated approval by silent hand gestures, snapping their fingers or standing to wave the flaps of their togas. Unlike today, violent applause was raised in disapproval, to 'explaudere', or drive the performers from the stage. With the sense of a violent eruption of noise, the term shifted to describe the result of the explosion of man-made powders, which 'drove away' the enemy.

FRANCHISE and FRANKFURTER

The early French, or Franks, took their name from the Old French 'franca', free, so those who speak 'frankly' do so without the hindrance of politeness, and 'franked' mail goes free of any further charge. The person holding a 'franchise' is free to exploit the area covered by that agreement and 'Frankfurt' grew up at the point at which the Franks crossed the river Main to do battle with the Germanic tribes – the Ford of the Franks. The aromatic olibanum brought home by Frankish Crusaders was called 'frankincense'.

Imported from Frankfurt, the mildly spiced sausage became a big hit in late-nineteenth-century America, where, sold in buns as finger food, 'hot dog' was applied due to the now-little-known German penchant for eating dogs, which gave rise to the not-entirely-humorous notion that frankfurters contained dog meat. Although it is common knowledge that dog is eaten in many Asian countries, the Germans too once had a liking for the 'delicacy', with the sale of dog meat not prohibited until 1986. The Swiss too are still tucking into thousands of cats and dogs every year with Hundeschinken, a kind of dried dog meat jerky, a great favourite. Cooked in white wine and garlic, cat is a festive dish served up at Swiss-Christmas and although the commercial sale of cat and dog meat is banned, in 1993 the Swiss Parliament rejected a bill calling for the ban to be extended to the slaughter of domestic pets for personal consumption.

FASCIST and FASCINATE

Both are derived from the Latin 'fasciare', to bind together with a band or sash.

In Ancient Rome the magistrates were always preceded by a man bearing a 'fasces', a bundle of wooden rods bound with red sashes, to symbolise the power of the united peoples of Rome. When they ventured outside the city, an axe head was incorporated into the fasces to warn all that the bearer brought with him the power of life and death. The axe head was rarely displayed within the bounds of Rome, where it was the people themselves who decided such matters. Either way, when Mussolini set up his political party in 1921, he resurrected the image of the fasces for a logo and named the party after it.

As for 'fascinate', this originally denoted the casting of a magic spell or curse that bound an individual to the sorcerer. Today, of course, the term is bandied about for anything of passing interest, with a 'fascinator' no longer being a witch but a skimpy head adornment worn by women at Ascot. There is also 'fascia', which properly denotes anything that binds and not a facing panel; the building tie made of bent wire is a fascia and the transition of use seems to have been occasioned by the advent of the motorcar dashboard, which was so called because it bound all the instruments and switches together, not because it presented a 'face'. Having undergone several spelling changes, 'basket', as originally made of interwoven wands of reed or willow, is also a distant relative.

FILLET and FUNICULAR

The Latin 'filum', a thread, gave its name to the 'fillet' that needs tying up before cooking, with 'filament' and 'filigree' close cognates. People line up in a 'file' and the office 'file' being named for the documents stored within that are attached by a string to the cover. A close relative in Latin of 'filum' is 'funis', a cord or rope, with the 'funicular' car taking its name from the cable that pulls it up the hillside.

FLAMINGO and FLAMENCO

Although today it might be difficult to imagine the Belgians as flamboyant and risqué, sixteenth-century Flanders was under the control of the Spanish, who did consider the 'Flamenco', as they called the locals, to be more than a little outrageous in both dress and behaviour. When the gypsy-style music and dance of Andalusia evolved in the late seventeenth century, they attracted the same name as both were considered a bit boisterous and 'Flemish' by Madrid.

It is worth mentioning that the southern Spanish region of Andalusia was originally named Vandalusia for its being colonised by that Germanic tribe as a jumping-off point for their invasion of North Africa.

That aside, it is easy to see why, when the Spanish first saw the flamboyant pink birds, they too were termed 'Flemish' for their garish appearance.

FLU and FLUSH

The Latin 'fluere', to flow, is the foundation here, with a person's 'influence' running through their social and political circles. Disease was in ancient times though to be caused by the influence that 'flowed' from the stars, and when a particularly virulent pandemic hit fifteenth-century Italy, the stars were blamed and the condition called the 'influenza'.

Obvious cognates are 'fluid', 'fluctuation' and things being in a state of 'flux'; 'fluorescent' light flows through the air; the 'affluent' are 'flush' with money while 'effluent' flows through the sewers and away from the city. Too much of anything is, of course, 'superfluous'. Also cognate is the 'flush' of the loo to form a 'confluence' with the effluent, and the poker 'flush' in which the run of the cards flows through the hand. A four-flusher is a cheat because the unsporting try to lay down a fake flush with the fifth and cheat card obscured by the four that are actually in suit or sequence.

FOCUS and CURFEW

'Focus' was the Latin for a fireplace, and in the days before the fifty-inch Cyclops that dominates our centrally heated living rooms it was the fire that was the focus of all in the room. 'Focus' arrived in Old French as 'fuier', to produce both 'feu', 'fire' and the 'foyer', which was a room at the front of house kept warm to greet guests. In the form of 'couvrefeu', cover-fire, the first 'curfew' was imposed in England by William the Conqueror and announced by the ringing of bells at 8 p.m. This was in part imposed to reduce the risk of fire in wooden buildings but was in reality more of a policing action aimed at reducing movement and keeping everybody indoors; once the fire was out in those days there was little else to do but turn in.

FORNICATE and FURNACE

As the population of Ancient Rome ballooned, the traditional one-man-one-oven bakeries were no longer viable and gave way to more commercial operations. These abandoned baking domes had a vaulted upper section, an archway known in Latin as a 'fornix', a term that also gave rise to the Latin 'furnus', an oven or 'furnace'. They do say that nature abhors a vacuum and human nature was quick to fill the voids of these abandoned ovens, as the city's prostitutes took them over as places of business.

Although 'fornication' has since the thirteenth century been used by the Church and moralists to denote sex outside marriage, the term did retain its original and architectural sense of vaulted archwork until the early 1800s, which makes sense of otherwise puzzling references to various bishops eulogising about 'exquisite fornication' in cathedrals.

FROGS and CRAPS

Although incognate, both owe their existence to the French 'crapaud', a toad.

The heraldic device of Clovis (d. 511), first king of the Franks, presented three toads, creatures then thought to possess magical powers, this later producing 'Jean Crapaud', or Johnny Toad, as a nickname for any Frenchman. In the lead-up to the French Revolution, the courtiers at Versailles, harking back to the glories of the Franks and considering themselves superior to the political rabble in Paris, thought of themselves as toads and the Parisians as frogs, frogs being the less imposing of the two creatures. 'Qu'en disent les Grenouilles?', or 'What do the Frogs say?', was a typical way of inquiring after the mood in the city; foreigners picked up the term and used it willy-nilly of any Frenchman. Thus the term has nothing to do with the French predilection for consuming the sturdy 'cuisses' of such creatures. (Actually it's more than just the thighs but it reads better on the menu.)

'Craps' is a variant of the English game of hazard, as named from the Arab 'al-zahr', the die, with the name of that game coming to mean a danger as the game itself was nothing if not 'dicey'. It was the French who introduced this game to New Orleans in the mid-1800s, where it was first known as 'Crapaud's dice' before 'Craps' and finally 'craps'.

G

GARNISH and WARRANT

Both the offspring of 'warn', the former was born of the transition of the Old Northern French 'warnir' to the Middle French 'gaunir' or 'garnir', all three meaning pretty much the same. Should a fortification be warned of impending attack the occupants would immediately set about 'decorating' their battlements with the usual paraphernalia of medieval defence, to be left standing 'garnished', as the term presented in English.

These were martial times indeed and victory for either defenders or attackers would be celebrated with a special meal, the centrepiece of which was usually the original blancmange, a term which is basically the French for 'white food'. Unlike the sweet dish it is today, the blancmange comprised rice, diced shallots, diced hard-boiled eggs and chicken, all moulded into outlandish shapes with aspic. The favourite display was that of a war tower standing garnished, complete with sugar models of soldiers and catapults, hence the transition of 'garnish' from the battlements to the kitchen.

The 'warrant' issued for arrest used to be a public proclamation warning all to shun the nominated party lest they be deemed guilty by association, and the original 'guarantee' warned the recipient of the kinds of actions that would negate the promise of safe passage. The original 'garret' was a lookout tower to give early warning of approaching danger so that the 'garrison' could stand ready.

GAY and NOSEGAY

One rarely sees nosegays these days unless watching judges in full fig marching in procession, when they are carried as a traditional reminder of the days when the judiciary kept a few such posies handy to ward off jail fever. These were the days when it was thought that disease was caused by foul odours – hence 'malaria', bad air – and that the 'gay', or light-hearted and pleasing, aromas of the flowers would afford protection. As for 'posy', this is a cognate of 'poem', with the original posy being a ring inscribed with a line of poetry as presented round the stems of a few flowers by wealthy beaux to their intendeds. The less well-heeled had to make do with just the flowers.

But to the downfall of 'gay'. Back in the 1600s a dissolute heterosexual man would have been called a 'gay fellow' and in the 1700s a woman who was either a bit promiscuous or a full-blown prostitute was said to be 'gay in the tail'. So an association between 'gay' and prostitution was well established by 1889, when the Cleveland Street scandal broke. This centred on a homosexual brothel run in that London street, which had some prostitutes as young as twelve and a list of clients, including Prince Albert Victor, son of the then Prince of Wales, that read like *Burke's Peerage*. The judicial elite has long been at pains to demonstrate how out of touch it is, with barrister Mervyn Griffith-Jones, leading the 1960 obscenity prosecution of Penguin Books for its publication of *Lady Chatterley's Lover*, asking the jury if it was the sort of book they would be happy for their servants to read, while Judge Pickles once halted proceedings to ask, 'Who are the Beatles?' It was a similar gaffe of Sir Thomas Chambers, presiding over the Cleveland Street prosecutions, that knocked 'gay' into its current usage.

One of the final witnesses, a male prostitute called John Saul, admitted under questioning that he had many friends who were 'gay', meaning 'on the game' but without any gender significance. With all in the court fully aware what Saul meant, Chambers caused a bit of a snigger by asking for clarification of the term, with the nature of the case ensuring that 'gay' would be thenceforth be linked to male homosexuality. The 'homo' element here is not the Latin one meaning 'man' but the Greek 'homo', meaning 'same', as in 'homogeneous' so lesbians could equally be described as 'homosexuals' but tend not to be. Perhaps the New York psychiatrist and gay-activist George Weinberg was unaware of this fact when he coined 'homophobia' in

1961 to leave his construct with the nonsensical meaning of 'a fear of the same'.

GAZETTE and GAZETTEER

To keep the citizens up to date with the never-ending wars with the Ottomans, the sixteenth-century Venetian authorities published a news-sheet that cost one 'gazetta', a low-denomination coin named from the image of a 'gazza', or magpie, on the reverse. As this was one of the first formally produced newspapers of regular issue, the term spread rapidly to other countries.

As for the geographical index called a 'gazetteer', this took its title from the first such publication, as issued in England in 1693 by the historian Laurence Echard, who named it *The Gazetteer's or Newsman's Interpreter*.

GENUINE and GENUFLECTION

Both derived from the Latin 'genu', knee, the meaning clear in the latter term, which denotes the dropping to one or both knees in a display of contrition or abeyance, but the explanation of 'genuine' is more complicated and starts with the biblical use of 'thigh' as a euphemism for 'penis'.

Although there are plenty of occasions where 'thigh' appears in the texts to mean thigh, there are examples of the euphemistic use, especially in Genesis, which at 24:2 reads: 'And Abraham said unto his eldest servant of his house, that ruled over all that he had, put, I pray thee, thy hand under my thigh and I will make you swear by the Lord, the god of Heaven, and the God of the earth, that thou shalt not take a wife unto my son of the daughters of the Canaanites among whom I dwell.' Later, at 47:29, we have Joseph required to do likewise to his father and swear not to bury him in 'Egyptian soil', while in both Genesis and Exodus the children of Jacob are described as being of his thigh. Perhaps this also explains why the Philistines were so wearied of being smitten 'hip and thigh'; the First Book of Samuel tells of David slaying two hundred Philistines and bringing back their foreskins to Saul as a dowry for the hand of his daughter, Michal, in marriage. How touching.

Throughout medieval Europe and until as late as the mid-eighteenth century consummation of royal marriages had to be witnessed to prevent either party trying to opt out the morning after with an annulment by claiming that no sex had taken place. This has led to countless stories of royal bedchambers filled with guffawing courtiers as the deed was done – but not so. All anyone had to see was the man touch the woman's body with his thigh, as in the upper part of his leg, and consummation was pronounced. Royal births were also witnessed to prevent substitution in the event of a stillbirth; after all was deemed proper, the father took the child before the court and placed it on his thigh to indicate it was of his seed. To the casual observer, perhaps unaware of the old biblical significance of this act, the child appeared to be on the father's knee and thus declared 'of the knee', or 'genuine'.

GEOGRAPHY and GEOMETRY

The former reflects the Greek 'geographia', a writing about the earth, while 'geometry' originally denoted the skill of measuring out parcels of land, hence 'geometrical', characterised by straight lines and right angles.

GERRYMANDER and GARLIC

Political shenanigans with county boundaries first got their name in 1812, when Elbridge Gerry (with a hard 'G'), the Democratic-Republican governor of Massachusetts, decided to redefine certain county boundaries within the state to give his own party the best chance in forthcoming elections. His redefined Essex County took on such a contorted shape that the opposing Federalists fancied it looked like a salamander and hired sympathetic artist Gilbert Stuart to lampoon the county boundary in cartoon by adding claws, wings and a head, and to publish the result under the title 'Gerrymander'.

With its hard 'G', Gerry is derived from the German 'gar', a spear, as indeed is 'Garry' and the name of the composer Elgar, or elf-spear. 'Garlic' is a hand-me-down from 'gar-leek', the leek with the spearhead segments, and the bull's horn was once called the 'gore', a term more often now applied to its effect on the unwary matador.

GHETTO and JETTY

In 1291 the city of Venice ordered that all the glass-making factories be moved to the island of Murano as a safety measure after a few disastrous fires. The abandoned quarter, known as the Ghetto, which was the Italian for a furnace or foundry, was later allocated to serve as the Jewish quarter of the city, complete with curfews and Christian guards on all access points after dark. As other European cities established their own segregationist areas, the term simply transferred.

At the root of 'ghetto' lies the Latin term 'jectare', to throw or cast, the former still used in pottery for the making of an item and 'cast' iron still made in a foundry. The sowing of seeds by walking through the field throwing handfuls hither and yon, was known as 'broadcast', a term adopted by the BBC at its foundation in 1922, as it saw itself scattering the seeds of knowledge in a similar fashion. The jetty 'throws' itself out into the water, as the modern 'jet' projects itself through the air. 'Jetsam' is thrown from boats, a 'jeton' is a token thrown into play in gambling, and 'conjecture' is an idea thrown open for discussion.

GIGOLO and SHEILA

The Middle French 'gigue' was a violin or fiddle and, by extension, a dance, whence 'jig', the 'jigsaw' with a blade that dances up and down to produce the puzzle of the same name, and 'jinks', be they high or low. In France the term was more closely associated with 'leg' – hence 'gigot' of lamb – so 'gigolette' emerged for the dancing girls of Paris who so frequently worked a street shift that the term drifted to mean 'prostitute', with the pimp living off their earnings being the 'gigolo', himself not averse to escorting lonely ladies who would expect to pay for any 'extras'. The link between 'leg' and sex is well attested, flighty women being known as 'a bit of leg', which prompted 'gig' to shift up the leg to the vagina, with 'jig-a-jig' or 'jiggy' still commonly understood to mean sexual intercourse and 'up your gig' (or 'giggy') a longstanding insult in both Britain and Ireland.

At some point in eleventh century, there emerged in France and Spain bizarre carvings on the walls of castles and churches presenting a crone-like woman squatting in the primitive birthing position with mouth agape and hands holding wide an exaggerated vagina; these are thought to have been representative of the cycle of life, with the crone devouring the dead and getting ready to issue new life. By the twelfth century these were seen on the walls of English churches too, as well as in Ireland, where, come the mid-nineteenth century, the carvings had acquired the name of 'sheela-na-gig', or woman with vagina. These can still be seen on early church walls or crouching in statue-form in the grounds, but, perhaps understandably, clerics of delicate disposition have planted strategically placed shrubs or climbing vines to obscure the figures. By the close of the nineteenth century over a third of the population of Australia was Irish and it was this flood of migrants who took with them 'Sheela' or 'Sheila', as applied to a girl seen only in the sexual context.

GRAMMAR and GLAMOUR

Both words are firmly rooted in the Greek 'gramma', a letter of the alphabet, and therefore close relatives of terms such as 'telegram' and 'programme'.

In medieval times, literacy was pretty much the province of the clergy and monks, and canny vendors of inks and paper would typically position themselves outside the local monastery door rather than wander from one market to the next, since anyone needing a letter written would have to beat a path to that door. As such vendors had no need to travel about they were called stationary shops, this spelling later altering to 'stationery', perhaps to avoid confusion. Thus it was that men of letters attracted a certain mystique; they were the celebrities of their time. Hard as it may be to imagine a bunch of scribes punching the air and screaming 'Pen, ink and rock-and-roll!', 'glamour', simply a ricochet of 'grammar', surrounded them.

With those involved in the occult and alchemy also being literate, 'grammar' in medieval times started to attach to witchcraft and other dark arts; the Old French 'gramaire' was routinely used in such context and in Scotland 'gramarye' was also put to such use. In early-eighteenth-century Scotland the variants of 'glamer' and glamor' emerged but still with a meaning of using witchcraft to delude people into seeing quality or beauty where none existed. The works of Burns and Sir Walter Scott are peppered with the use of 'glamour' in this context and, as late as the close of the nineteenth century, a woman described as glamorous would have been one using cosmetics and wigs to distract from the fact that she was rather plain. Not until the opening of the twentieth century did the term drift to its present position.

Interesting enough, these threads of witchcraft and cosmetics were drawn together by a Bill of 1770 proposing that any woman 'who seduced or betrayed into marriage any of His Majesty's subjects by the use of scents, paints, cosmetic washes, artificial teeth, false hair, Spanish wool, iron stays, hoops, high-heeled shoes or bolstered hips shall incur the penalty of the law in force against witchcraft'. Fortunately for some, Parliament rejected the Bill.

GRINGO and GREEK

Throughout the eighteenth and nineteenth centuries, the Irish migrated in their droves to the Americas, those from the north favouring New England while those from the south followed established trading links to South America. Argentina still has the fifth-largest Irish population of any country. Best known of these migrant families were the Lynches from Galway, whose scion, Ernesto 'Ernie' Lynch, became better known as Che Guevara.

But the Irish accent engendered unique problems when it came to the mastering of Spanish pronunciation in both South America and Mexico, another favourite bolt-hole for southern Irish migrants; actor Anthony Quinn was Mexican-Irish and the real-life El Zorro, or The Fox, was the seventeenth-century Irish adventurer William Lamport. Just as English has 'it's all Greek to me' to denote unintelligible speech or concepts so convoluted as to defy understanding, the Hispanics too used much the same expression to dismiss the verbally inept Irish, who were collectively ridiculed as 'the Greeks', or rather 'los Griegos', a term that, by the 1850s, had settled to 'Gringos'.

GROTTO and GROTESQUE

When early archaeologists explored the grottoes of Ancient Rome, some of the more outlandish murals depicting contorted sexual union upset their delicate sensibilities, so their coinage of 'grotesque' was adopted in general speech to denote anything unpleasant or distasteful. Casting around for a euphemism for some of the more animated sexual depictions, they settled on 'antics', based on 'antique', a term that has softened over time to meaning nothing more than harmless capers.

The Liverpudlian truncations 'grot' and 'grotty' were popularised by the Beatles.

GNOME and NORM

The foundation of the Greek 'gnome', intelligence or knowledge, produced 'gnomon', which could denote either a carpenter's square or the index on a sundial, both of which impart knowledge. 'Gnomon' is the most likely progenitor of the English 'norm', as first descriptive of a carpenter's square before it moved into metaphor to denote that which was considered 'normal'. It is worth mentioning here that 'enormity' denoted only aberrant behaviour that is outside the norms of society; basically the term means 'evil', not 'of massive proportions'.

The 'gnomes' are the keepers of the secrets of the earth and the creatures who know where all the treasure lies, so their name is allied to the 'gnostic' who thinks he knows the truth; the 'agnostic' who is unsure what the truth is; the doctor's 'diagnosis' and the 'prognosis' that foretells the development of the ailment; and the 'physiognomy', or the physical features by which you are known.

GOSSIP and GIDDY

As their time for giving birth drew imminent, women of early England would summon the appointed godmothers, or 'godsibbs', who would virtually take over the house and usher the men unceremoniously out of the door. There were godfathers too but they were more involved with the child in later life. In the view of the ousted menfolk, the female godsibbs or 'gossips', as they were known by the close of the sixteenth century, did nothing but prattle inconsequentialities.

Not unlike the dervishes of whirling fame, Christians of early England retained more than a touch of the pagan and were much given to incorporating wild dancing into their devotions. After flinging themselves around in circles they imagined the feeling of disorientation to be divine possession, and so called the state 'godig' or 'gydig', both meaning 'god-possessed', with the modern spelling of 'giddy' emerging at about the same time as 'gossip'.

GRAFT and GRAVE

'Grave' derives from the Old English 'grafan', to dig, hence also 'engrave', to etch or dig into. The special spade used for trenching and gravedigging was thus named a 'graft' or a 'grafter' and, with gravedigging being pretty arduous work, 'graft' or 'hard graft' emerged. With the grafter presenting a flat blade, ideal for skimming off the bottom of the grave, 'graft' meaning pecuniary corruption emerged in mid-nineteenth-century America to describe the activities of corrupt officials who kept skimming off public funds.

GRAPPLE and **GRAPEVINE**

Until the end of the eleventh century, grapes were known as 'wineberries' in English, the new term deriving from the kind of knife used to harvest them. Resembling a modern carpet-layer's knife, with a hooked blade sharpened on the inside curve, the 'grape' was a handy tool that also found a use on the battlefield, where it was ideal for hooking between plates of armour to inflict unpleasant injury. The 'grapple', or 'grappling hook', took its name from its similarity in shape. With vineyards now lined with 'grapevines' instead of wineberry tressles, the new term would much later find a place in slang as a direct result of the massive expansion of the telegraph network during the American Civil War. Rapidly colonised by assorted climbing plants, the poles supporting the network soon earned the telegraph the nickname 'grapevine'; if you 'heard it on the grapevine', it was most likely true.

GROG and **GROCER**

After Admiral William Penn – he for whom Pennsylvania was named – captured Jamaica in 1655, rum became the Navy's tipple of choice, with thick 95 per cent proof rum issued at the knee-buckling rate of half a pint per man per day until 1740, when Admiral Vernon put a stop to the Navy's floating party. His aide, Captain Lawrence Washington, oversaw the watering-down of the ration, which, unpopular from the outset, was nicknamed 'grog' because Vernon was known as 'Old Grog' for his boat cape made of the heavy material grogram, a corruption of the original French 'grosgrain', large or coarse weave.

Captain Washington was soon returned to his native Virginia, where, trading as a grosser, he establish an estate named Mount Vernon in honour of his old boss. The estate eventually passed to his half-brother George, who went on to bigger things, continuing to use Mount Vernon for presidential meetings. But Lawrence Washington was not a 'grocer' (modified spelling of 'grosser') of the high-street variety; he was a 'grosser' who bought in large quantities before selling to intermediaries such as the broacher, who tapped wine casks to sell small quantities to the man in the street; the title of 'broacher' survives as 'broker'. The grosser bought in multiples of 144, or a dozen dozen, hence 'gross', and as business at that level demanded one's full attention the metaphorical 'engross' emerged in the 1660s. Because 'gross' could also mean 'coarse and heavy', as early as the 1500s the term forked out into the realm of the unpleasant, vulgar and even immoral, so the habit of modern teenagers flouncing around denouncing anything they dislike as 'gross' is very old-fashioned indeed.

Getting back to the naming of Pennsylvania, most imagine it to celebrate the Admiral's son, William Penn, the founder of Philadelphia, but not so. As a Quaker, Penn junior could not accept eponymous honour and suggested the land be called Sylvania, for its forests; it was Charles II who insisted on the addition of 'Penn' to celebrate the victories of Penn senior over the Dutch.

HARBINGER and HAMBURGER

The German 'burg', the castle that accords safety and shelter to those within, and 'bergen', to bring to safety, are the main progenitors of these and several other terms.

His title based on the Old French 'herbergier', shelter for soldiers, the 'harbinger' of the fourteenth century was the officer who rode ahead of an army to arrange billeting for the officers and campsites for the rank-and-file. With the locals usually expected to foot the bill with good grace, it is fair to say that the only people pleased to see a harbinger were the innkeepers and the local 'anthology of pros', this imparting the negative overtones the term enjoys to this day. During the English Civil War (1642–51) Coventry played the unwilling host to a massive presence of Parliamentary troops and was taxed to the eyeballs for the privilege. The locals ostracised their unwelcome guests, not even speaking to them, resulting in a posting to that city seen as a punishment in Cromwell's army, hence being 'sent to Coventry'.

First settled in the ninth century when Old Saxon and not Old High German was the language of the area, Hamburg was likely named from the Old Saxon 'ham', which meant a river-bank or a riverside meadow, thus giving the settlement a name meaning the fort on the meadow. The American idea of a good steak has always been half a cow on a bin lid so when they saw German immigrants of the late nineteenth century mincing up perfectly good beef only to reform it into flat cakes they dismissed the concept as a 'Hamburg steak'.

Thus 'hamburger' started out as an insult, not unlike Welsh rabbit – never 'rare-bit' – or Welsh dresser, both of which imply poverty or low condition. The notion behind the former was that the Welsh could not even afford rabbit and had to make do with cheese on toast, and 'Welsh dresser' implied that Welsh women would doubtless be too poor to have dressing tables in their bedrooms and thus had to titivate themselves at the kitchen cupboard.

Allied terms are the French 'berger', who gives shelter to his sheep, the 'harbour' that gives 'lodging' to ships, and the 'burglar', who was originally a freebooter specialising in night attacks to loot small towns and forts. It is perhaps for this reason that, in British law at least, burglary only takes place at night; during the day such crime is termed housebreaking.

HARP and HARPY

Contrary to the modern image and use of the term, the Harpies started out in Minoan culture as funeral priestesses selected for their physical beauty; they stood attendance naked under the feathered cloaks that they wore to represent vultures, then regarded as psychopomps, or transporters of souls, as they devoured the dead before winging skyward. The Harpies' title was definitely based on the Greek 'harpazein', to seize or pluck, but it is not clear whether this was applied for the women representing a bird that plucked at the dead or for their plucking at harps (also from the same root) throughout a funeral; probably both. Given their associations with death it was perhaps inevitable that the Harpies would undergo a downward slide until mythologised as foul and winged demons sent to plague men. Until the seventeenth century the term could apply in metaphor to a person of either sex but after that time the term was reserved exclusively for women with an evil temper and/or a pronounced inclination to avarice.

HEARSE and REHEARSE

The Samnite 'hirpis', which also produced terms such a 'hirsute', meant 'wolf', and 'hearse' originally denoted a harrow with wolf-like teeth that was used to break virgin ground. In rural England, which in the Middle Ages represented the lion's share of the land, the farmers' triangular hearse was used to bear bodies to the church for burial – so this was definitely one wolf to keep away from the door. The term was also used for the triangular

89

metal frame holding tapers or candles to light the coffin as it lay in state. Interestingly enough, the Algonquin for 'wolf' was 'p'tuksit' which in turn gave name to Tuxedo Park, the 1880s playground of New York's petulant rich where the tailless evening jacket made its debut.

Also known since the early 1300s is 'rehearse', to describe the metaphorical ploughing over of the same ground.

HELICOPTER and PTERODACTYL

Both terms are linked by the Greek for 'wing' but only one of them actually flew.

One could build a reasoned argument for a silent P in helicopter; indeed many did refer to the early examples as 'helicoters' because the name was built of the Greek 'helix', spiral, and 'pteron', wing. This latter is the same element that appears in 'pterodactyl', and if the P is silent there why not equally so in 'helicopter'?

Although lost-world movies always include attacks by wing-flapping pterodactyls, these were not flyers but gliders, with a membrane stretching between their two 'little fingers' and their hind legs, hence the name translating as 'wing-finger'. Too heavy for proper flight, the pterodactyl could stay aloft all day on thermals and swoop down on prey, providing there was a glide path to follow after the attack. Any pterodactyl that got grounded had a very clumsy and undignified 'hike' to a point high enough for it to get airborne again.

HERMAPHRODITE and DYKE

Hermes, messenger to the Gods, had a dalliance with Aphrodite to produce a son called Hermaphroditos who, in a moment of madness, went swimming in a magical pond, as you do, only to find himself corporeally morphed with one of the playful nymphs. Hermes was of great significance to the early alchemists and when they found a way of locking substances in airtight containment, this was called 'hermetic' sealing. In American rural dialect 'hermaphrodite' was itself morphed into 'morphadike' to produce 'dike' or 'dyke' in the 1920s, to describe the kind of lesbian who presented a mannish persona, dressing in men's clothing and keeping her hair cropped.

Although it sounds apocryphal, there really was PC outrage when the Black Dyke Band announced their first visit to America, where the feminist lobby decried their name, unaware that the world-class brass band was named for its formation in Yorkshire's Black Dyke Mills and that the band was not a musical troupe of black-and-butch lesbians.

HERRING and HERR

The Middle High German 'her', whence the modern and respectful German 'Herr', meant 'old and distinguished' – grey-haired, if you like – and the 'herring' has a grey underbelly. The metaphorical 'red herring' is an allusion to a kipper being dragged along a trail to teach hounds to follow a scent, or, conversely, across a trail to put them off the scent. Thomas Nashe wrote in 1599 that 'to draw on hounds to a scent, to a red herring skin there is nothing comparable', and the first to use the expression in the deceptive sense was polemicist William Cobbett, who in 1807 wrote that he had tried the ruse to deflect hounds from their pursuit of a hare but that it had only a transitory effect. The American TV programme *Mythbusters* tried it with bloodhounds and found the same, so the expression only works in the realm of metaphor.

Interestingly enough, back in the 1500s 'kipper' denoted a smoked male salmon, so named for the 'kip' or horned beak the fish grows in the mating season; when herring became the cheaper option the term simply transferred.

HIPPOPOTAMUS and PENICILLIN

The common root here is the Indo-European 'pet', to attack or fly at, this producing in Latin 'penna', a feather or wing. The first 'pen' was but a sharpened quill requiring the scribe to keep handy his 'penknife' to re-point it. By extension, the Latin 'penicillus' was an artist's brush, whence the later 'pencil' and 'penicillin', a fungus bearing conidiophores with tufted or feathery ends – 'pennon', 'pennant' and 'penne' pasta are all cognates.

The original 'pet' also produced the 'competitors' who attack each other, the 'petulant' who are always sniping, the 'appetite' that attacks the stomach, the 'impetuous' who rush in without thinking, the 'impetigo' that attacks the skin, the 'petition' that instigates a legal attack, and 'repe(a)t', which originally meant 'to attack for a second time'. 'Pet' arrived in early Greek as 'pot' to create 'potamos', literally 'rushing water' but understood to mean 'river', with 'hippopotamus' bearing a meaning of 'river horse'; Mesopotamia is the land between two rivers.

The centaur, or more properly the hippocentaur, entered Greek mythology after the first encounters the horseless Greeks had with mounted Asiatic raiders whom they imagined to be a meld of man and horse. Their name comes from 'hippokentaurus', the horse that goads bulls. 'Kentron' meant any sharp point so, with the hippocentaurs being fabled bull breeders, this could be a reference to them keeping the herd in tight formation; equally, that second element could mean 'bull slayer' as the hippocentaurs were also fabled for their prowess with a bow – hence such a creature representing Sagittarius. Linked to the Greek 'kampos', a sea creature, we get the 'hippocampus' in the brain, named for resembling in shape the seahorse, and by linking 'hippo' to 'dromos', a running or a racetrack, we get 'hippodrome', originally a horse track, which in the late nineteenth century and for reasons unfathomable transferred to public theatres. That same 'dromos' crops up again in the name of the 'dromedary', or racing camel, and the old Roma 'drum', the local patch one runs around, and by extension one's abode.

And finally to the 'Hippocratic Oath' allegedly set down by Hippocrates, or Mr Horsepower, that second element being visible in terms such as 'democrat' and 'autocrat'. Either way the oath, if indeed written by Hippocrates, never contained the much-vaunted opening line 'First do no harm'. Though the physician does at least promise 'I will willingly refrain from doing any injury or wrong from falsehood, and (in an especial manner) from acts of an amorous nature, whatever may be the rank of those who it may be my duty to cure…' Things have moved on so much in the last 2,500 years that no doctor has taken the oath for ages and few even know its content.

HISTORY and STORY

In ancient cultures the 'histor' was the wise old man who kept first the verbal and then the written lore and legends of his people to hand down to the next generation. All history is a collection of 'stories' of varying accuracy, with 'story' transferring to additional levels of a building in the thirteenth century due to the trend of having external walls painted with figures telling a moral tale or 'story'.

HONKIE and HONKY-TONK

With the majority of poor Eastern Europeans arriving in nineteenth and twentieth-century America being of Hungarian origins, white people coined 'bo-hunk' or 'hunky' for all such immigrants, be they from Hungary or not. With implicit derogatory overtones akin to those expressed in 'white-trash', 'hunky' was eagerly adopted by Afro-Caribbean Americans in whose pronunciation it evolved into 'honkie'. In the Southern states a 'tonk' was a low bar or dance hall specialising in raucous music and carnal entertainment, and black people, more interested in blues or jazz, coined 'honky-tonk' or 'honkie-tonk' for such establishments and the kind of music played therein.

HOSTILE and HOSPITALITY

We have all likely been to parties where both of these have applied, which is fair enough in that the common root is the Latin 'hostis', a stranger, and an advancing 'host' was likely warlike, or an enemy. At the opening of the fourteenth century 'hospital' denoted a hostel offering 'hospitality' in the form of food and shelter to pilgrims and other strangers; the sense of a charitable institution tending to the sick and needy is not noted for another hundred years or so.

HUMOUR and HUMIDITY

Ultimately traceable to the Latin 'umor', fluid, 'humidity' is pretty straightforward in that it denotes an atmosphere heavy with moisture, but 'humour' takes us back to early medicine.

The ancients believed that there were four main bodily fluids or 'humours' and that their complex interaction could be read in the face – hence 'complexion'. Not only were these fluids believed responsible for corporeal well-being, they were also thought responsible for a person's temperament and state of mind. Imbalance in the blood made you 'sanguine'; too much yellow bile, or choler, and you became 'choleric' or ill-tempered and at heightened risk of developing 'cholera'; too much black bile, or melas choler, and you became 'melancholy'; and too much phlegm made one 'phlegmatic'.

HUSSY and HUSBAND

Both are simple spin-offs from 'house' but there is a shameful prejudice attached to the former. A simple contraction of 'housewife', the term was driven to its present meaning by those of supposedly higher birth presuming that a commoner's wife who tended house was bound to be open to sexual advances. Wives of middle-class peasants were addressed as 'prudefemme' and, as they were invariably dismissive of any such advances, the first part of their title fell to its present position in the language. So, as ever, women were damned if they did and damned if they didn't.

A 'house-bond', a man bonded to a residence with land and livestock – the care of which is still called animal 'husbandry' – was a good marriage prospect, unlike the lowly baccalarius (cowboy) he employed who would likely remain a 'bachelor', and whose status explains why 'bachelor' also applied to those in the lowest stages of knighthood as well as the lowest degree attainable from a university.

The original Latin 'vacca', cow, was also responsible for the 'vaccination' of cowpox as protection against smallpox, and the 'vaquero' who tends such animals.

IDIOT and IDOSYNCRACY

Things have not changed much in the political arena over the millennia, as 'idiotes' was but the Greek for a private individual; one holding no public office – a voter, if you like. A person's private and individual 'quirks' are named from the Greek 'idios', 'syn' and 'krasis', meaning 'one's own', 'with' and 'mixture' respectively. 'Idioms' are forms of speech unique to a group of people or a place.

IMBECILE and BACTERIA

The diminutive of 'baculum', a log or rod, the Latin 'bacillum', a staff or rod used for support, is at root here, with 'imbecile', rather unpleasantly, being a reference to the fumbling around of the frail without their supporting staff; as physical frailty is so often accompanied by impairment of the mental faculties, the term shifted in meaning.

'Bacteria' under the microscope look like a collection of little rods, and after 'baculum' had passed through Italian as 'bacchetta', it arrived as 'baguette' in France, where the 'baccalauréat' degree was originally presented scrolled between two wooden rods. Eric Partridge, the celebrated etymologist, builds a good case for 'embezzle' deriving from 'imbecillare', to render feeble, as does the 'embezzler' weaken an organisation from within. 'Debacle', meanwhile, was originally descriptive of the sudden breaking up of ice on a river, as if someone had removed an invisible bar or 'bacle'.

IMMOLATE and MAELSTROM

In Lady Morgan's obscure *France* (1817), there is a single reference to 'self-immolation' as meaning suicide by fire, but few people ever read this. Only since the 1960s in English has 'immolation', or 'self-immolation', carried strong overtones of suicide by fire due to the horrendous news coverage in 1963 of the Buddhist monk Thich Quang Duc so dispatching himself. Duc was protesting the persecution of Buddhists in South Vietnam and his was followed by a flurry of similar suicides in protest of the Vietnam War itself. The term is based on the Latin 'molere', to grind, which also produced 'meal'; prior to the horrific events mentioned above, the term in English meant only the sprinkling of ground meal over a sacrifice in a temple.

'Maelstrom' is based on the Dutch 'maelstroom', a grinding

stream, as first used of the Moskenstraumen off Norway's Lofoten Archipelago, a massive concatenation of dangerous currents and whirlpools. The term enjoyed limited use in English until the publication of Poe's *A Descent into the Maelstrom* (1841), which not only presented the misconception that a maelstrom was exclusively a whirlpool – and one presenting a funnel to the ocean's floor – but also that such phenomena are dangerous to shipping; there are no accounts of ships lost to whirlpools, maelstroms or other vortices.

INFANT and INFANTRY

Both come from the Latin 'fans', present participle of 'fari', to speak, which in the case of 'infant', unable to speak, is pretty straightforward. As for 'infantry', this was first used in sixteenth-century Spain, the country being rightly proud of having the first professional and standing army that Europe had seen since the Fall of Rome. The term was used of those who fought on foot to protect the rear and flanks of a knight, who, unlike his infantry, would have had a banner to proclaim or 'speak' his name. Spain also coined 'infanta' for royal daughters who, excluded from succession, were unable to speak on matters of state in court.

INFIRMARY and FARMER

The first 'farmers' were not the horny-handed sons of soil the term denotes today but rather the first tax collectors, who took their title from the Medieval Latin 'firma', a fixed payment. These founding fathers of the Inland Revenue would buy a county's tax-collection concession for a fixed amount from the lord of the shire and then try to tax a profit out of the locals; we still talk of sub-contracted work being 'farmed out'. The farmers worked hand-in-glove with the escheators, who valued estates fallen to Crown possession through lack of heirs, and their notorious fiddling produced 'cheat'. Come the mid-to-late 1500s, 'farmer' sidestepped to denote men who leased arable land for a fixed rent and then tried to profit from the crops they grew.

Naturally, the 'infirmary' is the place for those of weakened condition or those in whom others saw no value, as they were 'in-valids'.

INK and CAUSTIC

Most early forms of writing were burnt into wooden tiles in a process known in Latin as 'encaustum', to burn into; the favoured wood for written records was that of the beech tree, which, known in German as 'bok', produced 'book'. When the first inks were produced, 'encaustum' survived as their name, and when that moved into Old French it was decided that the first element only would suffice; 'enque' moved into Middle English as 'inke'.

Obvious cognates are 'caustic' and 'cauldron' and 'holocaust', from the Greek 'holokauston', something that is entirely consumed by fire – a sacrifice to the gods. It was in this sense and with various spellings that the term enjoyed sporadic use in English from the twelfth century, with the *OED* listing a quote of 1648 in celebration of 'the perfect holocaust of generous love'. One of the first to use the term in anything like its present meaning was Churchill writing after World War I of the Turkish-inflicted genocide of the Armenian peoples; by 1938, the term was infrequently used of the Nazi atrocities inflicted on the Jews and other 'undesirables'. Not until the 1960s did this become the prime meaning, although the victims themselves often opt more for the Shoah, or the Calamity, and the Hurban, or the Great Destruction.

Today there are many Jews who object to the use of 'Holocaust' as a synonym of 'Shoah' or 'Hurban' because of its pure meaning of a sacrifice offered up to please the gods.

INSPIRE and PERSPIRE

The notion that a person's breath, or 'respiration', embodies their very 'spirit' and that corporeal health is inexorably linked to spiritual well-being is a very old one. The act of breathing in 'inspired' the individual and the link to the spirit shifted 'expire' to mean 'to die'. Those who breathed together in cahoots 'conspired', while 'transpire' properly means 'to perspire' or 'to breathe through'. That last term has fallen to a meaning of 'to reveal or occur', a usage deemed misuse by the OED and other purists, but methinks that is a battle long lost.

Ordinary breathing patterns were thought safe in medieval England but any sudden exhalation was feared to eject the spirit or soul from the body, hence 'God bless you', which has nothing to do with the Plague, as popularly imagined, as there was no violent sneezing to mark the onset of the condition. In the Hindu culture, for example, it is customary to clap the hands loudly in front of the mouth after sneezing to frighten the spirit back into the body.

Interestingly enough, 'bless' itself has a grim past in that it originally meant 'to cause to bleed through violent injury'; 'blesser' as a verb in modern French still holds such a meaning. The shift was occasioned by pagan priests slitting the throat of a sacrificial animal before collecting the blood to 'bless' the congregation with bloody thumb prints to the forehead. Prior to giving this 'blessing', the priest would dip the tips of his thumb and first two fingers of his right hand into the blood and kiss them to indicate that all was as it should be, some maintaining that this is the origin of the Mediterranean gesture of excellence. As the gesture is known to be at least 2,000 years old, this suggested origin could indeed be correct.

INSULT and SALMON

Both come from the Latin 'saltus', a leap, with 'insult' having swapped meanings with 'injury'. Allied to 'jury' and even 'conjurers', the magicians who 'con-jure' or collectively swear to keep secret the tricks of their trade, 'injury' in the sixteenth century meant 'to swear and curse at someone' – to vilify them. 'Insult' then meant 'to leap on' them and give them a good beating, which makes sense of 'to add insult to injury', to escalate things: first shout at them and then beat them up. This original meaning is reflected in the legal concept of 'assault', which actually applies to verbal harassment; 'battery' is added if the incident escalates into physical violence.

The 'salmon' is famed for its abilities to leap upstream to spawn; 'somersault' is an obvious sister and the 'desultores' of Roman circuses were the equestrian acrobats who specialised in leaping from one horse to another on the gallop, hence 'desultory'. Although now a tad outmoded, 'to sally forth' in attack is an allied usage, as is the name of the 'Aunt Sally' at the fair, a figure for all to attack at will.

INTERNECINE and **NECTAR**

'Internecine' was first seen in *Hudibras* (1663), a satirical poem by the English writer Samuel Butler in which this was his rendering of the Latin expression 'internecinum bellum', a savage war characterised by wholesale slaughter. Nearly a century later, Dr Johnson decided to include the term in his *Dictionary of the English Language* (1755) but, misunderstanding the first element of Butler's construct to be the same as 'inter' as in 'international', he gave the term's definition as 'striving to mutual destruction', which is pretty much how the term is used today.

In fact, this 'inter' is an intensifier so an internecine action can be all one-sided; Hitler's Holocaust was most certainly an internecine action.

The origin lies in the Latin 'nec', based on 'nex', violent death, which also gave us 'pernicious', 'noxious' and 'obnoxious', the latter two derived from the Latin cognate 'noxa', harmful injury inflicted with murderous intent. Also cognate are the less-heard 'nocent', those capable of harm or murder, and the more-heard 'innocent' and 'innocuous', who are incapable of harmful activity.

The gods of the ancients sustained their immortality by drinking 'nectar', the second element, 'tar', meaning 'overcoming', whence the nectar of flowers and the delicious 'nectarines' giving a juice thought worthy of the gods. The food of the gods was ambrosia, named from the Greek 'ambrotos', immortal, and the crumbs that fell into their laps while dining were imagined to fall to earth as opportunities for mankind when they stood up, hence 'in the lap of the gods'.

INTOXICATE and TOXOPHILY

Both come from the Greek 'toxon', a bow, and the Latin 'toxicare', to smear an arrow with poison.

All early poisons were distilled from plant life and the first to be 'intoxicated' were those shot to death with poisoned arrows. When the ancients began to distil more interesting fluids from plant life the term simply transferred.

JADE and ILEUM

The Spanish acquired from the Moors the belief that a piece of jade strapped to one's side would cure kidney infections, so the stone was named 'piedra de ijada', stone for the side, which moved into French as 'l'ejade' before corrupting in error to 'le jade'. The other name for jade, 'nephrite', derives from the same medical myth in that it derives from the Greek 'nephros', a kidney. 'Ijada' is ultimately rooted in the Latin 'ilia', the side or the groin, hence the intestinal 'ileum'. As for 'jaded', worn out, this comes from the wholly separate Old Norse 'jalda', a mare, but especially one worn out through excessive breeding.

Although incognate, 'effete' is synonymous in that, a close cognate of 'foetus', it first applied in the seventeenth century to any animal worn out through excessive breeding before transferring to boredom-feigning fops of the mid-nineteenth century.

JANUARY and JANITOR

Always portrayed with two faces so that he could look both ways, Janus was the Roman god of doorways and, by extension, of opportunities, especially in war. The Romans saw him as responsible for what they saw as the 'magic of war', whereby inexplicable events could suddenly turn the tide of fortune on the field. During times of war his temple doors were left open so he could intervene as and when he saw fit; they were closed in times of peace in case he decided to start something.

In his role as protector of doorways he gave name to 'January', the door to the new year, and the 'janitor' who has the keys to all the doors in any one building. Those of devious nature are still called 'Janus-faced'.

JARGON and GORGEOUS

Late-fourteenth-century English adopted the French 'gorge', throat, whence 'gorge' denoting a ravine, 'gorge', to eat in a voracious manner, 'disgorge', to vomit, and 'gargle', to make a noise in the throat – whence 'gargoyle', a hideous visage on the side of buildings with mouths agape to act as drainage spouts. Originally presenting as 'gargon', 'jargon', somewhat pleasingly, originally denoted the inane twittering of birds. Although the term is of infuriatingly impenetrable origins, is it not possible that 'argot' it somehow allied to 'jargon'?

Inspired by the intricate lace neckpieces then worn, 'gorgeous' appeared in the fifteenth century when some of the most elaborate and expensive examples were sold at St Audrey's Lace Fair at Ely. So much that is quality gets debased and St Audrey lace, or 'Tawdry lace', was no exception, leading 'tawdry' to its current status.

JOCKEY and JACKET

Poverty and bad diet have long afflicted those living beyond Hadrian's Wall, this resulting in stunted growth and rickets, a condition marked by bandy legs. This made Scotland, where 'Jock', a variant of 'Jack', was and still is a common name, a happy hunting ground for seventeenth-century riding stables to find lightweight riders, or 'jockeys', for English bloodstock. It was this same dietary deficiency that later prompted the Germans to call Scottish soldiers, especially the Glaswegian Cameronians, or the Scottish Rifles, the Giftzwerge: the Poison Dwarves.

Although 'Jack' is commonly held to be the pet form of 'John', it is more properly that of 'James', deriving as it does from the French 'Jacques', which is in turn derived from the Middle Latin 'Jacobus', the progenitor of 'James'; the supporters of James VII of Scotland (James II of England) were the 'Jacobites'. The French peasantry has long been known as the 'Jacquerie', and in the fourteenth century such men tended to wear a short and tight-fitting coat, or 'jacquette', which arrived in English in the mid-1400s.

The garment was subsequently adopted by women in a

modified style and, called a 'petticoat', it was used to suspend underskirts from hooks about its lower hem; when underskirts were made with drawstrings the need for the bodice-like petticoat disappeared but the name remained attached to the underskirts themselves.

K

KAISER and CAESARIAN

The *OED* states a caesarean section to be 'the delivery of a child by cutting through the walls of the abdomen when delivery cannot take place in the natural way, as was done in the case of Julius Caesar', but no matter how popular this proposed etymology is, it is simply not plausible.

The Lex Caesaria, or Law of the Cut, was passed in Rome in the time of Numa Pompilius (715–673 BC), long before the birth of Julius in 100 BC. The law required any woman who died in advanced pregnancy or in labour to have the child cut out for separate burial. Thus in Rome it was only performed on dead women, whereas Julius Caesar's mother is known to have been alive when he began his tour of the British Isles. Of course, in the case of a woman dying in labour, it is probable that some infants did survive the trauma; and as Julius was by no means the first of his clan to bear the cognomen 'Caesar' it is possible that an ancestor thus survived to start the cognomen.

After he had crossed his Rubicon to take power, his cognomen became a title, as did that of Cleopatra, with 'kaiser', 'czar' and 'tsar' all derivatives.

KARAOKE and KARATE

Long and rightly famous for their exquisite forms of torture, the Japanese first exported 'karaoke' to the United States in 1961, from where it spread across the Atlantic to invade Europe. The Japanese themselves have a lasting love affair with Western classical music and, given the cacophonous twanging of some of their more traditional genres, this is perhaps little wonder. But they had no word for 'orchestra', so they adopted that too as 'okesotora'. 'Kara' in Japanese means 'empty' or 'missing' and, blended with 'oke', they coined 'karaoke' – an empty or missing orchestra.

Martial-arts films peddle the myth that 'karate' was a medieval Japanese skill developed by peasants who, banned from carrying weapons, wanted to punch through the bamboo armour of the Samurai. With a name meaning 'empty hand', karate was actually developed in the Ryukyu Islands and not introduced to Japan until the 1922 visit of Gichin Funakoshi (1868–1957), revered as the Father of Karate.

KAZOO and BAZOOKA

Both of these words derive from the Dutch 'bazuin', a trumpet, which in early-nineteenth-century American slang had morphed into 'bazoo', the mouth or a loud bluster. Warren Frost, American inventor of the raucous instrument, tried to patent his 'bazoo', as it was initially called, but was told by the Patent Office that the term had already fallen into the public domain; re-filing on 9 January 1883, he opted for 'kazoo', now somewhat appositely American slang for the anus.

The origin of 'bazooka' is more complicated. American musical comedian Bob Burns claimed to have invented the musical bazooka as a thirteen-year-old in 1903 when, messing about in his local plumbing shop in Arkansas, he fitted a bell funnel to a length of pipe and played it. But Arkansawyer farmers had for decades been using something strikingly similar to sow seeds in long furrow without bending over all the time. Armed with a bell funnel and a length of flexible pipe, the farmer walked along with a shoulder bag of seed, which was fed into the funnel and allowed to fall from the trailing pipe.

When the farmers downed tools for a party – hence 'hoe-down' – these seeders would be played in much the same way as did Burns in his popular act; to be fair, though, he did coin the name by blending 'bazoo' with the then-popular Russian suffix 'ka', as in 'babushka' and 'palooka'. Burns and his bazooka were still popular in World War II, when American troops thought the sound of a projectile leaving the launch tube of their anti-tank weapons reminiscent of the noise generated by Burns. The

Germans called their similar weapon the Panzerschreck, tank fright, that last element now firmly associated with the rotund, green, CGI-movie monster.

KNICKERS and KNACKERS

Both of these are rooted in terms such as the Middle High German 'knacken' or 'knicken', to crack, and the Swedish 'knaeka', to rap together. Obviously the path of 'knickers' is more convoluted than that followed by 'knackers'.

The trail starts with Washington Irving's *A History of New York from the Beginning of the World to the End of the Dutch Dynasty* (1809). Intended to be an affectionate burlesque on the lives of the early Dutch settlers of New Amsterdam, as the city was first named, Irving chose to write under the equally frivolous pen name Diedrich Knickerbocker, a surname denoting the baker of children's marbles, known in Dutch as 'knickers', for the rapping sound they make when striking each other in play.

Generally truncated to *Knickerbocker's History of New York*, the book was illustrated by George Cruikshank and featured all the early male characters in the kind of traditional Dutch costume that included highly coloured 'plus-four'-type trousers. As these looked pretty similar to the voluminous women's underpants of the day, such bloomers soon acquired the nickname 'knicker-bockers', and when the garments became smaller so too did the name. The 'Knickerbocker Glory' ice cream was named because the colours of the various ingredients were thought reminiscent of the multicoloured silks in those same illustrations.

The testes became the 'knackers' in crude allusion to their rapping together as the owner ran along, perhaps carrying his personal effects, or 'knick-knacks', in a sack in which they all rapped happily together.

The 'knacker' who came to take away 'knackered' horses to the glue factory was identifiable by the distinctive rapping sound his cart made on the cobbles. The wheels were heavily cleated to prevent slipping beneath such a heavy load. Also related is the Dutch 'knappen', to crack together or bite, and by extension to eat, and although 'knapsack' is today but a synonym of 'rucksack' or 'backpack', it began life denoting the sack a cavalryman carried to store oats for his horse.

KNUCKLEDUSTER and KNOUTY

Brass knuckle guards are noted in antiquity, with the gladiators calling them the 'cestus', but 'knuckleduster' itself emerged in the mid-to-late 1800s in America with the advent of compact and composite weapons comprising a six-shot pinfire pistol with a folding set of brass knuckles that could either be opened out to form the handle of the barrelless pistol or be used on their own to seriously batter an opponent. 'Knuckleduster' arose in reference to the fact that, if fired, the gun would 'dust' the owner's knuckles with powder burns. In Paris such guns were known as 'Apache pistols' through their use by the underworld thugs of the same name, who are still celebrated in a cabaret dance act in which a thuggish man hurls and slaps a woman about with violent disdain. When the guns faded from use the term remained for any brass knuckles.

'Knuckle' is derived from the Middle Low German 'knokel', a bone or small bump, so 'knuckle' is cognate to 'knot' and 'knitting', which is but a series of knots. Also linked is the Russian 'knout', a whip with knotted lashes that was used to brutal effect by the Cossacks and the Black Hundreds against Russian famine-protesters in the lead-up to the Russian Revolution. As did 'bolshy', from 'Bolshevik', enter English slang at that time to describe anyone truculent and intractable, so too did 'knouty', to describe those irascible to the point of violence.

KYKE and KU KLUX KLAN

Odd bedfellows indeed here, in that the former were always a target of the latter, but both derive from the Greek 'kuklos', a circle or a group of people united in a common aim.

The society of hooded murderers was spawned on Christmas Eve 1865 in Pulaski, Tennessee, after the close of the American Civil War, by a small group of disenchanted Confederate officers determined to maintain the status quo. Mainly of Scottish heritage and otherwise well educated, they adopted the name from 'kuklos' plus 'clan', which was given a K to maintain alliteration. Interestingly enough, this was the first example of the satiric replacement of C with K, a device that was readily adopted by supportive Southern businesses in their advertising before spreading across the States and the UK to be used by other firms ignorant of the origins or significance.

As for the Klan's burning cross, this too has its roots in Highland history. Forever at each other's throats, the Scottish clans were summoned to unity against a common enemy by a runner carrying the Crann Tara, or Fiery Cross; it was also known as the Cross of Shame as calumny would be heaped on any ignoring its call. Thankfully now a spent force, the Klan's only remaining 'blemishes' on the American landscape are the massive carvings on Georgia's Stone Mountain and South Dakota's Mount Rushmore, both carried out by Gutzon Borglum (1867–1941), a high-ranking Klansman.

As for 'kyke' or 'kike', according to Philip Cowen, founder and publisher of *The American Hebrew* and Leo Rosten, Yiddish lexicographer and author of *The Joys of Yiddish* (1968), this was born on Ellis Island, around the turn of the twentieth century. The influx of poor and illiterate Eastern European Jewry into the United States refused to sign their papers with a cross, deeming this too 'Christian' a symbol, so they opted instead to sign with a circle. Cognate to the Greek 'kuklos', the Yiddish 'kikel', also meant a circle with the derivatives of 'kike' or 'kyke' first used by established and more educated Jews of their less-fortunate brethren before it was latched onto by general American usage and applied derogatorily to any Jew.

These 'kikel-writers' would be taunted in the streets by children making circular motions with their index-fingers in the air, a gesture which, later made to the side of the head, intimated stupidity or even insanity.

115

LABYRINTH and LABIA

The latter is taken direct from the Latin for 'lips' and thus needs no further explanation.

'Labyrinth' was properly the name of the original labyrinth allegedly built by Daedalus for King Minos of Crete, who needed a place to house the Minotaur, the hideous offspring of his wife's dalliance with a white bull – those Greeks certainly knew how to party! The Minotaur was fed on criminals and those who displeased Minos, and over the entrance to their doom was carved an image of the 'labrys', the Cretan battleaxe which, with its two curved blades, resembled a pair of lips.

The Minotaur was finally killed by Theseus, who laid down a reel of string on his way into the Labyrinth to make sure he could get out again; the popularity this story in late medieval England forever changed the meaning of 'clue', which had previously only described a ball of thread or string. Semantically speaking, it is wrong to confuse a labyrinth with a maze or to regard the two terms as being in any way synonymous. The maze presents navigators with successive choices of paths, some of which lead to dead ends, while the labyrinth has only the one path leading to its centre – so Theseus did not actually need his ball of string but perhaps he did not know that when he entered.

LAVENDER and LAVATORY

The Middle Latin 'lavare', to wash oneself, has also produced the 'lava' that washes down from an erupting volcano, the 'laver'-bread made from seaweed washed ashore, the 'lather' that is generated by washing and 'lavish', as first descriptive of torrential rain. Fragrant 'lavender' was anciently used to freshen up baths or to fold into 'laundry' to keep it fresh until required.

The English language has long been coy about words that denote a room in the house dedicated to the purpose of evacuating waste from the body, and has thus found itself in constant need of hijacking washing terms to use in euphemism. Until the mid-1880s, 'lavatory' meant only a bowl in which to wash or the room set aside for such a purpose; some in 'polite' society still announce their need to go and 'wash their hands'. Derived from 'abluere', to remove by washing, 'ablution' has fallen to much the same usage.

Previously, a lady at her 'toilet' was at her dressing table, typically covered with 'toile', a kind of linen, washing and putting on her make-up before dressing. Rubens' *Venus at her Toilet* and Degas' *Woman at her Toilet* both depict such scenes.

LIBIDO and AD-LIB

The second term is a truncated form of the Latin 'ad libitum', (to extemporise) at one's pleasure, with the first leading the person so possessed to pleasure, or disaster, as is more often the case.

Synonymous with 'ad-lib' are 'off the cuff', a reference to Victorian speakers keeping short notes scribbled on the stiff shirt cuffs that were then in fashion, and 'off the top of your head', which has more modern origins. In the early days of American television, a producer anticipating a gap in the running time would indicate this to the presenter by patting himself on the head and holding up a number of fingers to communicate the number of minutes the anchor was expected to fill with 'off the cuff' chit-chat.

LIKE and LYCH-GATE

The Old English 'lic', a body, produced 'like', in that most bodies do look alike, with 'like' in the sense of 'affection' arising to describe the emotion felt if you liked the look of someone's 'lic'. In terms of probability, 'likely' first applied to those who looked strong and able before moving on to describe possible events that seemed capable of translating into a reality. The covered gateway with benches at the entrance to a churchyard was built to store coffins for burial in the event of the priest not being available when the dead arrived. It is a body-gate, if you like.

The distant cousin 'ilk' is today somewhat misused to mean 'similar' or 'alike', whereas it is only properly employed to denote a nobleman residing on the estate of the same name. 'Lord Stanley, of the ilk' means the Lord Stanley residing on the Stanley Estate, as distinct from any other Lord Stanley in the realm.

LIMELIGHT and LEMON SOLE

The Latin 'limus', mud, slime or any sticky mess, produced terms such as 'birdlime', a glue smeared on branches to trap birds, hence 'doing bird' for penal servitude, an expression no doubt helped by 'birdlime' offering a nice rhyming slang for 'time'. Through the sense of smearing with such a substance, 'lime' was extended to the calcite used to produce plaster, mortar and, let down in water, to whiten woodwork, especially 'limed' oak; dark or blackened oak was achieved with horse urine. It would not be until the 1830s that anyone thought of burning lime to produce the powerful white light that revolutionised stage lighting, with the Cornish magician Ching Lau being the first to 'step into the limelight' on 3 October 1836 at Herne Bay Pier Theatre.

'Slime', 'slick', 'sleek' and 'loam' are fairly obvious relatives but so too is the 'lemon' sole which, although delicious with citrus accompaniment, was first known as 'limen/limon sole' for its frequenting the muddy bottom of the sea. 'Sole' is the same word as applied to the base of the foot, in allusion to the fish's flat profile and shape.

LOGGERHEADS and BACKLOG

Inspired by the Latin 'lectus' and the Greek 'lekhos', both meaning 'bed', 'leggen', to lie down flat, arrived in Middle English and quickly inspired other terms such as 'legge', a bar or flat 'ledge', and the 'ledger' in which records are laid down. 'Logge' soon followed to describe a felled tree that just lay on the ground and, through several spelling changes, the 'law' that is laid down also emerged.

'Backlog' has shifted from meaning something useful to something irksome, as in the fifteenth century it denoted the heavy wooden log at the back of a domestic fire that was used to keep other combustibles to the fore, where they could render the most heat to the occupants of the room. Not until the 1930s did the term come to be used of an unaddressed amount of work.

As for 'loggerheads', this is certainly of naval origin but which of the two loggerheads is responsible is unclear. On a seventeenth-century man-of-war, 'loggerhead' could describe either a kind of double-cannonball shot, the two being joined by a metal bar so they resembled the weightlifting bar hoisted by circus strongmen, or a wooden pole with a metal 'log' at one end that could be heated to melt and spread pitch on the decks. The former was only used at very close quarters, to whirl about the enemy deck causing mayhem, and the other was frequently used by sailors to sort out differences. Either could have inspired 'at loggerheads'.

Dutch and Low German coined 'legeren', to camp, especially in the military sense, so a town that was 'beleaguered' was one under siege. In later German, 'Lager' denoted either a military camp or a storehouse, hence the 'lager' beer that needs storing longer so all the sugar can turn to alcohol. The eternally rerun *The Great Escape* celebrates the mass escape from Stalag Luft III, more fully 'Stammlager Luft', or Main Camp for Aircrew.

LOMBARDY and LUMBER

The Longobardi, Late Latin for either 'the men of the long beards' or 'the men of the long axes', were a Germanic people who invaded northern Italy in the sixth century to establish what is now called Lombardy. By the Middle Ages they were heavily involved in the European moneylending business, with London's Lombard Street, if now only historically, the city's banking district. 'Lombard' was commonly rendered 'lumbard' or 'lumber', and if you were in hock (from the Dutch 'hok', jail) to the Lombards then you were also said to be 'in lumber'.

The pawnbroker's sign of three golden balls is thought to be linked to a heraldic device used by the Medici family, once-powerful Italian moneylenders and bankers.

LOOPHOLE and LUPUS

Although the term is most often used today to denote an escape route in a legal document, the original 'loophole' was the vertical slit in a castle wall for the archers to fire through. The masonry on the inside was chamfered to widen the angle of fire and so took its name from the Middle English 'loupe', to peer out slyly from ambush, as does a wolf. The ultimate source is of course the

Latin 'lupus', a wolf, and the unpleasant medical condition was named for its 'devouring' healthy tissue like a ravenous wolf. Also kindred is the 'lupine', a flower that, like the wolf, can survive in hostile conditions.

It is said that W. C. Fields, a life-long atheist, was found reading the Bible on his deathbed, claiming he was looking for a loophole; but in reality his last words, far more in keeping with the man, were, 'Damn the whole fucking world and every son-of-a-bitch in it except you, Carlotta' – this to his companion, Carlotta Monti, with him to the end.

LUCIFER and LUNATIC

It is incorrect to identify Lucifer with Satan; the Bible makes no such connection as the name Lucifer appears but once in the whole book and does so in derision of Nebuchadrezzar II (sic), the haughty king of Babylon who had been boasting that his throne would shine like a light in the heavens. Crowing over the fall of Babylon, Isaiah 14:12–15 reads, 'How art thou fallen from Heaven, O Lucifer, son of the morning', applying this name as it simply means 'light-bringer'. The confusion with Satan must be comparatively recent as there was a Bishop Lucifer of the fourth century who is still venerated as a saint in Sardinia.

That said, it is unlikely in the extreme that any church would sanction the christening of a child with such a name, yet there seems no prejudice attached to the female forms of Lucy, Lucinda or Lucille, all of which, like Lucifer, ultimately derive from the Latin 'lux', light. It should also be said that it is only in films specialising in spinning heads and copious amounts of green vomit that Satan is identified by 666; the so-called Number of the Beast is 616 and always has been.

Also traceable to 'lux' are terms such as 'illuminate', 'lustre', the bright and shining 'luxury' we all seek from time to time and, of course, 'lunar', as descriptive of the shining moon once thought to influence the insane, hence 'lunatic'. Remote cousins are the 'lynx' with its bright and shining eyes and 'leukaemia', a condition marked by an excess of white blood cells.

LUMBAGO and HUMBLE PIE

The Latin 'lumbus', loin, gave its name to the 'lumbar' region of the body and the 'lumbago' that can afflict it. There are several silly stories of various monarchs being so fond of loin of beef that they knighted it Sir Loin, but the term comes instead from the French 'sur-loigne', over or above the loin. That said, it seems that in the mid-eighteenth century a group of clubmen, believing the Sir Loin stories to be true, christened a double sirloin left uncut at the backbone a Baron of Beef, as that rank is one step up the peerage from a knight.

Known in Old French as the 'lombles' or 'lumbles', the offal of a deer, located in the lumbar region, were usually given to huntsmen to make a pie while the lord and his cronies scoffed the venison. Known in English as 'umble pie', this was changed to 'humble pie' by folk-etymology through associations with lowly status. Increasingly, 'eating humble pie' is heard in the sense of people seeking forgiveness or making atonement.

As for 'offal', that denotes the bits that 'fall off' the carcass when it is initially cut into in a process known in the butchery trade as the dressing, a possible origin of 'a good dressing down' as denoting a cutting reprimand. 'Dress' was also used of meat cut and presented in shops, a possibly inspiration for 'mutton dressed as lamb'?

M

MAGGOT and MARGARINE

The Greek 'margaron', a pearl, not only created the name Margaret but also gave its name to the butter substitute first produced in an acceptable form in France in 1869 and properly termed 'oleomargarine' for the pearl-coloured fats used in its manufacture. The 'margarita' cocktail presents a pearly-coloured liquid and the pizza was first served in Naples in 1889 to mark the visit of Margherita, Queen Consort to Umberto I. The 'maggot' has a pearly appearance and the Scandinavian cognate 'mawk', maggoty, produced in English 'mawkish', riddled with sickly sentiment.

Birds were often given human names and in the early 1600s the pie was called 'margaret', or 'mag'; the culinary pie, with its mixed ingredients, was named after the pie bird which, mistakenly, was thought to be a thief that gathered various stolen trinkets together in its nest. The bird's plumage also created terms such as 'piebald' and 'pied', as in the Pied Piper of Hamlin, noted for his multicoloured outfit.

MANGLE and MANGONEL

The Germans have always been unnaturally fond of war, frequently giving their weapons affectionate and female names such as 'Gunhilda' (whence 'gun'), a term the Germanics first applied to the mangonels they used in order to hurl rocks at the enemy in the days before artillery. These machines ultimately took their name from the Greek root 'mang-', which could be used to refer to a sexually fascinating woman or to trickery and deception effected through sexual advance. Those Germans really knew how to get their rocks off.

Anyway, the erstwhile washday device was operated not by a geared wheel, as seen on later versions, but by a lever that was cranked to and fro on a ratchet, reminiscent of the similar crank-and-pulley set-up used to pull back the firing arm of the mangonel, so the weapon's name transferred as 'mangle' or 'little mangonel'.

Another Germanic sexualisation of military equipment shows in their greatcoat being known as Mathilda, the 'girl' who kept the owner warm at night. When not worn on hot marching days it was carried like a bedroll on a piece of string across the back, where it bounced from side to side as the owner marched along – 'waltzing Matilda' was a military term for a long hike and an expression that German migrants took with them to nineteenth-century Australia.

MAP and APPLE-PIE BED

English abounds with examples of a process known as false splitting or junctural metanalysis, which involves the N from 'an' attaching itself to the noun that follows. 'An ekename' became 'a nickname'; 'a nadder' became 'an adder'; 'a numpire', a word indicating that the judge had nothing to do with either of the contesting 'pair', became 'an umpire'; and 'a napron' became 'an apron'. The original 'nap' or 'nappe', linen, produced obvious cognates such as 'nappy', 'napkin' and, less obviously, the 'nape' of the neck which looks flat like ironed linen. The cognate 'mappe' or 'map' attached to charts as they were at first drawn out on linen for durability.

'Nappe pliée', folded linen, was corrupted in English to 'apple pie', as in 'apple-pie order', all neat and tidy like folded linen awaiting use, and the 'apple-pie bed', with the bottom sheet folded up and over the top sheet so the butt of the joke cannot get into the bed. 'Pliée' is cognate to terms such as 'multiply' and the 'pliers' originally used by metalworkers to fold hot metal.

MASTIFF and COMMANDO

The Latin 'manus', a hand, has imposed wide influence on English, with 'manacle' and 'manage' perhaps obvious cognates, while the well-'mannered' are pleasing – or 'hand-some' – a political party hands out its 'manifesto', those in 'manacles' might be 'emancipated', and those handed back to custody by a court are on 'remand'. 'Manure', rather unpleasantly, was once worked into the soil by hand, and 'Maundy' Thursday was once marked by the monarch handing out money to the poor. 'Manus' also produced 'mansuescere' in Latin, to mean 'to tame', or 'to get an animal used to being handled', so from the prefix 'mas-' we get 'mastiff' and also 'masturbate', to agitate by hand.

Orders are handed out by 'mandate' and the first troops to be given an open mandate to operate autonomously were the Boer Kommando, units that fought guerrilla actions as, when and how they saw fit. These units led Kitchener such a merry dance that the British army lost some of its starch to form similarly unorthodox units. As for 'going commando', this was first seen in print in the 1960s, which indicates a prior verbal currency and jibes with the suggested link to the World War II nickname for London prostitutes: Piccadilly Commandos. The mechanics of their trade would render knickers but a hindrance and the term was most certainly used of women for years before it applied to men. The term was certainly picked up by American airmen based in the UK during the war, as indicated by the names of two of the B24s flying out of southern airfields, one called *Piccadilly Lilly* and the other *Piccadilly Commando*.

In South America this risqué way of avoiding VPL is called going 'a lo gringo'.

MEDITERRANEAN and TERRIER

The Latin 'terra', dry land, is also responsible for the 'terraced' houses that share a common plot of land, the earthenware 'tureen', used for cooking, and the 'terra cotta', or baked earth, that is used in the manufacture of tiles; 'biscuit' started out in Italian as 'biscotto', twice-cooked, the means of removing sufficient water to ensure a longer shelf life. The herb thought worthy of planting was known in Middle Latin as 'terra merita', this arriving in English as 'turmeric'.

'Terra firma' seems almost a tautology save for the fact that it was first used by the Venetians in 1605 to denote the part of mainland Italy under their control – their Domini di Terraferma being thus distinguished from their watery powerbase. As such, the designation is similar to the proper meaning of the 'Spanish Main', which, although it denoted Spanish possessions on the South American mainland as opposed to those in the islands offshore, was believed in general English to denote a body of sea. The Romans thought themselves the focal point of the civilised world and so called their local sea the Mediterranean, the centre of the earth, and the Greeks thought much the same of their own waters, which they named from 'arkhi', chief, and 'pelagos', sea, later Italians taking 'archipelago' and applying it to any island-studded reach of sea.

As for the 'terrier', such dogs were bred for their diminutive stature, allowing them to get into burrows and badger setts to 'disinter' the prey.

METAPHYSICAL and METAPHOR

'Metaphysical' has been hijacked by the 'there are more things in Heaven and earth' brigade who, like many others, use it to denote that which is supernatural or ethereal, but this is a gross distortion of the term.

After Aristotle had written his *Physics*, he went on to publish *Metaphysics*; with 'meta' meaning 'after' or 'beyond', the title indicated the book to be a follow-on from *Physics* – *Physics 2*, if you like. The book dealt with substance and reality, causation, form and matter and mathematical constructs, but because 'meta-' could mean 'beyond', those who had never even read the book 'misinterpreted [it] as meaning the science of things transcending what is physical or natural', to quote the *OED*.

'Meta-' could also mean 'over' so, blended with the Greek 'pherein', to carry, 'metaphor' describes a word that shifts meaning over onto another word or expression; 'meteor' describes an astrological phenomenon that passes over us; 'metathesis' occurs when letters 'jump over' each other to change places in a word; blended with the Greek 'ballein', to throw, whence 'ballistics', we get the 'metabolism' that is constantly throwing one change over another in the body. 'Metamorphosis' is a changeover to another form; in the fingers the 'metacarpals' are located over or beyond the carpal bones of the wrist, as do the 'metatarsals' extend beyond the tarsal bones in the foot. Finally, blended with 'hodos', a pathway, we get the 'method' as established by going over the same routine again and again, to get 'methodical'.

MEWS and COMMUTER

The common link here is the Latin 'mutare', to change or alter, this producing the Middle French 'mue', a moulting of birds of prey or the shedding of antlers by deer, which moved into English as 'mew'. In either case the animals were undergoing change. Birds of prey are not really air-worthy in moult so trained falcons and hawks were kept in what were called mews until they had grown new plumage. So if you have just spent a fortune to buy a 'bijou' residence with a desirable London postcode only to feel trapped in a birdcage – you are!

This thread of change continues through terms such as 'immutable' and 'permutation', with prison terms often 'commuted'; a regular traveller on a specific route buys a season ticket to get a reduced or commuted fare to become a 'commuter'. 'Mutual' agreements alter the relationship between two parties, so two people can have mutual (or reciprocal) feelings of love or hate but they cannot have a mutual acquaintance, a popular error presented in the title of Dickens's last completed novel, *Our Mutual Friend* (1865).

MIRROR and MIRACLE

When the first 'mirrors' were produced – examples of obsidian mirrors have been unearthed in Anatolia and dated to 6000 BC – they were thought a 'miracle', with both terms linked by the Latin 'mirari', to look at with wonder, to 'admire'. Looking at themselves in a mirror for the first time, the first thing people did was to 'smile', a term English adopted from the Old High German 'smieron', to smile, which was itself also based on the Latin 'mirari'. With women making more use of such handheld miracles, the female symbol of a circle atop a cross is meant to represent a hand mirror.

Another close relative is 'mirage', which does not denote a hallucination experienced in the desert, as shown in so many films; rather it denotes mirror activity on a grand scale. The refractive index of air alters with temperature and when a mass of warm air meets cooler air the interface works like a massive mirror in the sky, allowing a view of what is over the horizon.

MONEY and MANIAC

In 390 BC the Gauls attempted a night attack on the citadel of Rome, but noise from their hefty wooden overshoes ('galoshes' – the Gaulish shoe) as they scaled the walls roused the geese sacred to the temple of Juno. The garrison turned out and sent the barbarians packing; Juno was awarded the additional title of Moneta or Myneta, She Who Warns, and the geese were slaughtered for a celebratory meal. Where's the justice in that?

Anyway, in 269 BC that temple to Juno-Moneta was used to house the Roman 'mynet', now 'mint', and the coinage issued named from Moneta. At the root of 'Moneta' sits the Latin 'mens', the mind, those with the right 'mentality' always staying alert, while the 'de-mented' are otherwise. The cognate Greek 'menos' produced 'mania' and 'maniac', with the element '-mancy' attaching to forms of divination – 'necromancy', or whatever – in which the mind of the 'reader' is guided by external influence.

MORRIS DANCING and **MAURITANIA**

Wishing to invade Spain, the Moorish warlord Tariq (d. AD 720) first established a powerbase in the Iberian island he called Jibal al Tariq, the Rock of Tariq, whence 'Gibraltar'. Once entrenched, the Moors held great sway in Spain for centuries but the Spanish nobility refrained from intermarriage and thus kept their pale skin with the veins showing blue, hence 'blue-blooded'.

But the point as far as we are concerned is that the Moors were still very much in evidence during the doomed fourteenth-century expeditions into Spain mounted by John of Gaunt (now Ghent). And as if military failure were not enough, in 1387 he brought back the strangely disturbing tradition of the 'morris dance', inspired by the 'Morisca danza', the Spanish name for the Moorish warriors' two-handed sabre dance in which those who lost the rhythm were likely to lose assorted body parts too. The silly little sticks that morris dancers 'fight' with are reminders of these sabres, while morris dancers additionally used to 'black up' until more recent times, when such antics became decidedly non-PC.

The ultimate root of both the name of the Moors and their powerbase of Mauritania is the Greek 'mauros', black, an origin that has spawned many mistakes, such as the aforementioned and quite unnecessary blacking-up of morris dancers, and white actors hamming it up like Al Jolson in a bed sheet to play Othello. Those of black skin are to be found in sub-Saharan Africa; the Moors of the northern coastal regions are essentially

Arab-Berber peoples with almost European features and lightly tanned skin. The eighteenth-century Scottish explorer Mungo Park, the first make it through to Timbuktu, recorded that his life had been saved on more than one occasion by his being mistaken for a Moor.

As for Othello, Shakespeare could have got it double wrong in that the character might not even have been a Moor. There is some suggestion that the inspiration for the character was Maurizio Othello, a white Venetian mercenary who had spent a considerable time fighting in Hungary, where the tradition is to place the surname first. The Hungarian for 'Morris' is 'Mor', so reference to 'Othello Mor' *might* have led Shakespeare astray.

MORGUE and ORGULOUS

The former is, surprisingly, quite unconnected with terms such as 'mortuary'; both arrived in English care of the French 'orgueilleux', presenting a proud and haughty demeanour. The latter was the first arrival, noted in print in 1250, and stayed close to its original meaning in French, as indeed it still does. 'Morgue' did not follow until the early seventeenth century, when it landed, initially at least, with synonymous meanings.

Meanwhile, back in France, the term had been taken up by the penal institutes to denote the induction wing for new inmates who were to be scrutinised for any signs of proud defiance that might mark them out as a problem once turned loose in the main body of the prison. The somewhat dramatic shift in meaning came in Paris in 1821, when the authorities opened up a 'viewing room' to display all the unclaimed dead of the city – suicides, bodies fished out of the Seine, and so forth – for anyone to wander in and check over the 'inmates' in case their lost loved ones were there.

Through the associations of looking and observing, the old penal slang transferred but better survived in America than it did in the UK, probably through the success of *The Murders in the Rue Morgue* (1841) by American gothic writer Edgar Allen Poe. Far more common in the UK is 'mortuary' which comes direct from the Latin 'mors', death as indeed does the onerous 'mortgage', Old French for 'dead-pledge'. This grim-sounding description of the arrangement is rooted in the fact that should the borrower default and the property be repossessed, all the money thus far paid is 'dead' to the borrower who walks away with nothing.

MUSKET and MOSQUITO

The fourteenth-century Italian 'moschetto' denoted both the sparrowhawk and the crossbow, since the early firearms were initially used to fire arrow-like projectiles, and the term made the transition into weaponry before entering English as 'musket'. It is always a puzzle that screen adaptations of *The Three Musketeers* almost invariably show the eponymous protagonists fighting with swords with nary a musket in sight! But no matter; the stinging 'mosquito' was named for its being imagined a minisparrowhawk; the so-called 'Mosquito Coast', on the other hand, is a misnomer born of a corruption of the name of the Miskito Indians who inhabited the area.

N

NAVE and NAVVY

Maritime symbolism was rife in early Christianity; the Pope is said to wear the shoes of the fisherman – Christians still sport fish symbols on their cars – and in the Middle Ages churches were perceived as ships of calm in a sea of doubt, which is why the main passageway to the altar is called the 'nave', from the Middle Latin 'navis', a ship. It should be said here that no bride walks up or down the aisle, unless she is completely lost, as the aisles of a church, named from the Latin 'ala', a wing, are the minor passageways to either side of and running parallel to the nave. In pure terms, 'ala' meant a point of articulation, so cognates of 'aisle' are 'axilla', or armpit, 'axis' and 'axle'.

The canals that formed the veins of the Industrial Revolution had to be dug out by labourers who were labelled 'navvies' because the canals themselves were at first called 'navigations'. From the cognate 'nautes', a sailor, we get terms such as 'astronaut' and 'cosmonaut', the 'nausea' experienced by those first at sea and the 'noise' made by a load of sea-sick passengers moaning, 'ad nauseam', about the weather and conditions.

Although more earthbound, 'juggernaut' is kindred to 'astronaut' in that the term is a European corruption of 'Jagannath', an avatar of the Hindu god Vishnu. Every year since the opening of the eleventh century, a massive statue of the god has been dragged in procession from its temple in Puri, on the Bay of Bengal, on a wooden cart of staggering proportion. The festival was first witnessed by Europeans in the early 1600s, who, marvelling at the way the statue was navigated through the crowded streets and focusing more on the cart than the statue, had by the 1700s corrupted the god's name into 'juggernaut', which within a century was being used of any massive machine or organisation.

NAZI and IGNITION

Few on the left of the political spectrum like it said, but many consider Hitler to have been a demented leftie, leading, as he did, the National Socialist German Workers' Party. No one who fancied a quiet life spoke of 'Nazis' in Hitler's Germany, as this was an insult coined by the Jewish journalist Konrad Heiden just before he sensibly fled Berlin for America. Party members called themselves National Socialists and shot anyone who called them Nazis.

Heiden was quite clever in his choice of insult, as 'Nazi' was and still is the rural Bavarian pet form of 'Ignatius', a name used of dunderheads and fools; Hitler himself was a Bavarian-Austrian who did not assume German citizenship until 1932. In turn, Bavarian slang selected 'Nazi' for such ironic use as Ignatius, meaning 'the fiery one', was also the name given to what is known in English as a will-o'-the-wisp. A little-understood phenomenon even now and properly called 'ignis fatuus', foolish fire, this is the illusive fire or luminescence seen dancing about at night on marshland. So 'Nazi' is a close relative of 'ignition', 'igneous' and 'ignite'.

NEIGHBOUR and BOOR

The Boer Wars fought in South Africa between 1880 and 1902, between the British and the Dutch/German settlers of the Cape, stirred up ill feeling on both sides. 'Boer' is simply the Dutch-Afrikaans for a farmer and in the form of 'boor' had seen sporadic use in English for any unrefined rustic, but the aforementioned conflict saw a rapid resurgence of that usage in the late nineteenth century, with the term surviving in that context.

A variant of 'nigh', the 'neigh-bour' was originally the nearest farm; New York's infamous 'Bowery' was named for its occupying the land originally taken up by the farm belonging to Peter Stuyvesant, a prominent citizen of New Amsterdam, as the city was then known. Stuyvesant protected his domain from the local hostiles with a stockade wall that ran along the line of what would later become Wall Street.

NIGGARDLY and **NIGGLING**

Both are linked by the Old Norse 'hnoggr', miserly or giving nothing away, but while 'niggling' has enjoyed a calm and peaceful existence in the language to describe, for example, feelings or doubts that are so vague that they are next to nothing, 'niggard' has lived a life of shame through misperceived links to 'nigger', with the most famous misunderstood usage being that of David Howard in a mayoral committee meeting in Washington, DC.

On 15 January 1999, Howard dismissed the proposed budgets of mayoral aide Anthony Williams as 'niggardly', which immediately brought howls of protest and formal complaints from Marshall Brown, a black aide who was also present. As if anxious to prove that the lunatics really had taken over the politically correct asylum, even after dictionaries had been consulted Williams accepted Howard's resignation.

Although roundly dismissed as being of wholly obscure origins, it is hard to ignore the possibility that 'inkling' is somehow linked to the above.

NONCHALANT and **CHAUFFEUR**

Early cars were steam-powered, so the driver had to double as the stoker to keep the boiler hot, thus taking his title of 'chauffeur' from the French 'chauffer', to make something hot; this in turn was built on the Latin 'calefacare', meaning pretty much the same, with 'facare', to make, seen in countless terms ranging from 'benefactor' to 'manufacture'. Thus 'chauffeur' is a close cognate of the 'chafing dish' that keeps food hot and the 'chafe', or friction burn, that the enthusiastically amorous so frequently get from carpets.

That same Latin root of 'calere' could also mean 'to be hot' in the sense of ardour or concern over an issue or problem – to burn with desire or indignation, if you like – so the impassive were said to be 'nonchalant', as in cool. Youngsters today may think it cool to lounge about pronouncing things to be 'cool' but that usage dates back at least to the 1500s and possibly beyond. Of equal antiquity is the notion that the innocent are free of heat, hence someone deceptively affecting the demeanour of innocence and looking as if butter wouldn't melt in their mouth.

A close cognate of 'calere' is 'calorie', which is actually a unit of heat with one thousand calories, or a kilocalorie, being the amount of energy required to raise one cubic centimetre of water through one degree centigrade. 'Calorie' has been hijacked into confusion by the food industry with waist-watchers perhaps unaware that the industry routinely uses 'calorie' instead of 'kilocalorie' on labels, so a chocolate bar professing to contain but 250 calories will in fact contain 250,000 such units.

NOON and NOVEMBER

'Noon' is a simple variant of 'nine' and in medieval times corresponded to 3 p.m.; people started work at 6 a.m. and had lunch at about 11 a.m., that term originally denoting a labourer's mid-morning snack, with the first main break at 'noon', nine hours after starting. It was much the same on the continent, where people also started work at 6 a.m., but due to the heat they took a rest at the 'sexta hora', the sixth hour, or the 12 noon we know today, hence 'siesta'. A close cognate of 'siesta' is the navigator's 'sextant', with its brass calibration arc at the bottom being one sixth of a circle.

Those in the local castle or manor house liked some entertainment before their noon meal at 3 p.m. Starting at perhaps 1.30 or 2 p.m., these performances included short plays and other forms of entertainment provided by jesters; when the day became less arduous and noon shifted into its present position, such entertainments found themselves stranded in the afternoon but still called 'matinees', as they had traditionally been performed in the morning.

The old Roman year began in March, so 'November' was originally the ninth month; the long-established Catholic service of the 'nones' still marks 3 p.m. as it did in the old days.

OCTOPUS and OEDIPUS COMPLEX

The Latin 'pes' and 'ped' and the Greek 'pod' and 'pous', all meaning 'foot', have produced several English words.

Well known is the legend of Oedipus unwittingly killing his estranged father and then marrying his mother, but less well known is the fact that his name means 'swollen foot'. Forewarned that his newborn son would one day kill him, King Laius of Thebes pierced the infant's ankles and tied both feet together before sending a servant to take the child into the mountains and leave him to die. Luckily for Freud, Oedipus was found by the ubiquitous kindly shepherd, who raised him to fulfil his destiny. As for the 'octopus', this is something of a misnomer in that the creature does not have eight feet but six legs and two arms (some argue eight arms).

Obvious allies are 'pedestrian', 'tripod', 'expedition' and the 'impediment' that stops progress, but less obvious are the 'pawn' that moves one step at a time and the 'repudiation' of a charge that is 'kicked back' by the accused; 'pedigree' derives from the French 'pied de grue', the foot of a crane (bird), which resembles the spreading pattern of a family tree. On the geographical front there is 'Piedmont', at the foot of the mountains; the 'Antipodeans' whose feet touch the earth from the opposite direction to those in the Northern Hemisphere; and 'Patagonia', or Land of the Big Feet, so named by early Spanish explorers who thought there be giants there.

OK and KINDERGARTEN

There must be more false etymologies hung about the neck of 'OK' than any other English word or expression. There are indeed some indigenous American tribal terms such as the Choctaw 'okeh', it is so, which missionaries of the 1820s mention being used by their native converts instead of 'Amen', and African slaves are recorded using the affirmative acknowledgement of 'kay' as early as the 1780s, but these are coincidental, with 'OK' first noted in nineteenth-century Boston.

On 23 March 1839, the editor of the Boston *Morning Post* wrote a satirical piece about the non-existent Anti-Bell Ringing Society, in which he announced that: 'The Chairman of the Committee on Charity Lecture Bells is one of the deputation and perhaps if he should return to Boston, via Providence, he of the Journal, and his train-band, would have his "contribution box" et ceteras, o.k. – orl correct – and cause the corks to fly, like sparks, upward.' This emerged at the height of an editorial fashion in the city for humorous acronyms with some, like 'OK', deliberately misspelled, as indeed had been its predecessor 'OW', orl wright.

The trend spread to New York, where editorials and other articles were peppered with the likes of 'KG', no good, 'KY', no use, as in 'know youse', and 'NSMJ', nuff said 'mong gentlemen. The silly trend was mercifully short-lived, with all ultimately swept away except 'OK', which was saved from obscurity by the unsuccessful attempt at re-election in 1841 of President Martin Van Buren. Born in the village of Kinderhook, New York, he was widely known as the Kinderhook Fox or Old Kinderhook, this last epithet being tied to 'OK' during his abortive run. Banners proclaiming that all would be OK with OK in office, or whatever, saved 'OK' from the linguistic scrapheap.

The augmented 'A-OK' was born of a misheard transmission from astronaut Alan Shepard to NASA Control in May 1961. Shepard denied ever saying 'A-OK' but admitted he might have mumbled 'Errr . . . OK' at some juncture; but by the time he was back on earth NASA press officer Colonel 'Shorty' Powers had already launched the misheard version to the press.

As for Kinderhook itself, the village's name is but the Dutch for 'children's corner', a name bestowed in 1609 when the crew of the Dutch carrack *Halve Maen*, or *Half Moon*, the first ship to arrive at what is now New York Harbor, noted the gaggle of native children assembled on the headland to watch the fun.

Believing that children should be nurtured like plants in

a garden, Friedrich Frobel opened his first 'Kindergarten', or children's garden, in the German village of Bad Blankenburg in 1840. Thanks to his focus on teaching his preschool charges the skills of social interaction and manners more than facts and figures, the concept was readily taken up across Europe and the United States.

ORCHESTRA and CHORUS

In the ancient world dancing seems to have taken precedence over singing, with the pit in front of a stage given over to dancers who interpreted what was being enacted behind them. Named from the Greek 'orkheisthai', to dance, this area was eventually taken over by musicians who claimed the same name.

The crossover thread continues to link terms such as 'choir' and 'Terpsichore', the muse of poetry and dance; most confusing of all, while every song has a 'chorus', that term is derived from the Greek 'khoros', a place enclosed for dancing, and 'chorus girls' are the rank-and-file dancers in a production. Equally, the 'carol' that is today sung was once danced and likely named from the Latin 'choraula', the flautist who played for the dancers.

ORIENT and ABORIGINE

For those of us in the West, the 'Orient' has always been the Land of the Rising Sun – 'Sol Oriens', as it would present in Latin, or 'Nippon' in Japanese. Thus the East was the point of 'origin' of the sun, and with solar positioning being so important in navigation and early surveying, 'orientation' emerged in the early nineteenth century to describe the process of establishing one's position by the position of the sun.

From the Latin 'ab origine', the initial rising or beginning, we get 'aborigine', but it is a mistake to assume this a term referring exclusively to the native population of Australia. The first people to be so called were the Latini of Central Italy (circa 1000 BC), so all Australian natives are Aborigines but not all aborigines are Australian. One could equally describe a native Glaswegian as an aborigine, but indulging in such semantics on Sauchiehall Street at closing time might prove painfully unwise.

OSTRACISE and OSPREY

The formidable power in the talons of the hunting bird inspired the Romans to call it the 'ossfraga', or bone-breaker. After passage through Old French as 'ossfraie', the term landed in English as 'osprey', which is thus allied to terms such as 'fracture', 'fraction', 'fragile', the fragile 'frangipane', and 'suffrage', as voting was in ancient times cast on small bits of broken pottery, bone or seashell – which takes us neatly to 'ostracise'.

Once a year in ancient Athens, the citizens were entitled to vote out of the city anyone they believed unworthy of remaining, even those in power who had become so popular as to present a danger to the status quo. Each voter made their nomination on an 'ostracon', a piece of shell or a pottery shard, and anyone who attracted 6,000 votes or more was given ten days' notice to quit the city for the next ten years under pain of death for an early return. Both Aristides and Cimon are known to have suffered such exile, with the latter recalled a few months early to broker a peace deal with Sparta.

PALACE and PALISADE

After Christian activists started the Great Fire of Rome in AD 64
– it wasn't Nero – many of the luxury residences on the Palatine
Hill were destroyed, so Nero took advantage of the situation
to build his OTT Dominus Aurea, or Golden House, in that
location. This was the first to be called a 'palace', named for its
location on the hill that was once defended by a 'palisade' of
sharpened stakes.

Obvious cognates are 'impale' and 'pale', from the Latin 'palus',
a fencing post. Alluding to an imaginary fence surrounding the
areas, the English established two 'pales', one in western Ireland
in the late Middle Ages, and another around Calais after victory
at Crécy in 1346, hence 'beyond the pale' to describe dark or
immoral shenanigans.

PAMPHLET and SYPHILIS

Believe it or not, both of these have poetic origins in the Greek 'philos', loving, with the former derived from an erotic poem entitled *Pamphilus, seu de Amore* (*Pamphilus, or Concerning Love*). Incredibly popular, it was churned out by scribes who sold the sheets in inns or on the street, causing the first word of the title to morph into 'pamphlet', which was used of any handbill or flyer.

As for 'syphilis', this was originally the protagonist of a pseudo-medical work entitled *Syphilis, sive Morbus Gallicus* (*Syphilis, or the French Disease*), published in 1530 by the Veronese doctor-poet Girolamo Fracastoro. The French, of course, called it the Italian or Neapolitan disease. Syphilis was an ancient shepherd-swineherd who cursed the sun god Apollo because it was too hot, only to have his insolence rewarded with the new disease. His name was intended to be a blend of Latin for 'swine-lover' and a nod to Sipylus of Greek mythology, the grandson of Tantalus, who was shot to death by one of Apollo's arrows, thought to be the progenitor of all plagues.

PANTHER and TREACLE

Although 'panther' has long existed in English, there is no such animal, the term used instead of black jaguars, black leopards and even in the USA of the cougar, which, confusingly, is never black in colour. That said, the term came to us from the Latin 'panthera', which seems to hold a meaning of 'all wild beast', which is probably as good a description as one can get of any cat so named.

The second element of 'panthera' comes from the Greek 'therion', a wild beast, which entered Latin as 'fera' to produce in English terms such as 'fierce' and 'feral', showing that the corruption of 'th' to 'f' – as in the modern trend for 'free farsand' instead of 'three thousand' – is nothing new. 'Therion' in Greek also produced 'theriake', a thick and herbal balm applied to bites from snakes and wild animals. This moved into Vulgar Latin as 'triacula', on through Old French as 'triacle', and thence to English as 'treacle'; the old sense is still visible in what is now called the Treacle Bible of 1549, which asks, at Jeremiah 8:22: 'Is there no treacle in Gilead?' instead of 'balm'. With the medicinal treacle being thick and viscous, by the opening of the seventeenth century the term started to apply to substances such as molasses.

The notion that 'like cures like' is a very ancient one indeed and early medicinal treacles frequently included some element of the animal that had caused the injury. In the event of the most common such injury, a dog bite, some of the recalcitrant cur's fur was blended into the treacle to make a poultice, hence the liquid 'hair of the dog' imagined to cure a hangover. The earliest known reference to 'hair of the dog' in connection with drunkenness is found in a text unearthed in Ugarit, now Ras Shamra in modern Syria, and dated to the close of the second millennium BC.

PANTIES and PANTECHNICON

Supposedly martyred in the Diocletian persecutions of AD 303, St Pantaleon, or All-Lion, was also known as Pantalaimon, Compassion for All, but it is the former name that mainly concerns us here. When the Venetian commedia dell'arte found itself in need of the ultimate 'boo-hiss' character, it created a cowardly miser and gave him the incongruous name of Pantaleon, who had by then become one of the city's favourite saints. Easily identifiable by his voluminous, harem-style pants, his name arrived in sixteenth-century English as 'Pantaloon', a term that soon referred exclusively to such trousers; the truncated forms of 'pants' and 'panties' becoming female-specific at the start of the twentieth century.

An interesting historical footnote attaches to St Pantaleon's more compassionate epithet of Pantalaimon, which was the name the crew gave the Battleship *Potemkin* after their famous mutiny of 1905, not that it did them any good. The last surviving mutineer, Ivan Beshoff, moved to Dublin in 1913, where, somewhat incongruously, he opened a fish and chip shop, dying there in 1987 at the age of 104.

There were other characters sharing the Venetian stage with Pantaleon; Pulcinella, the duplicitous Lord of Misrule, was assimilated into English theatre as Punchinello, who, with his long-suffering wife, Joan, evolved into Punch and Judy.

In 1830 a group of London businessmen opened a massive emporium in Motcomb Street, off Belgrave Square, to sell everything from furniture to fine arts, naming their venture The Pantechnicon, from the Greek 'pan', all, and 'techne', art. They had to build outsized panel-sided carts to deliver the furniture, ultimately bestowing the venture's name on all future removal vans. Obviously the link here is 'pan', so kindred terms are the

152

'panic' that could beset man and beast in the countryside at night when the eponymous mischievous deity came out to play, and 'pandemonium', all the demons, as coined by Milton in his *Paradise Lost* to describe the principle city of Hell. Far from the bawdy farce it is today, 'pantomime' was originally a mimed play of a religious nature. The 'panacea', meanwhile, is a medicine presented as a cure for all ailments.

PARADISE and PARQUET

Although now reserved for a heavenly setting, the original 'Paradise' provided far more earthy pleasures. The Greek 'paradeisos', an enclosed garden, emerged in Persian as 'paridaiza', to describe an enclosed hunting park or pleasure garden in which the Persian nobility got up to all sorts of indulgence.

The descendant 'parricus', an enclosed area, cropped up in Medieval Latin to later produce the Italian 'parco', the Spanish 'parque' and the French 'parc', with its diminutive of 'parquet', which in the sixteenth century was applied in France to those parts of a royal residence that were no-go areas for lesser mortals, or that part of a legal complex reserved for judges only. In either case, the fashion was to have the floor laid in a distinctive block pattern so interlopers were immediately alerted to the fact that they had ventured where they would not be welcome.

PARROT and WIG

These are linked by the name Peter, derived from the Latin 'petra', rock, and both are thus sister words of 'petroleum', rock-oil, and 'petrified', so scared as to be turned to stone, and names such as Perrier and Perron.

The first parrots brought to medieval France were nicknamed 'pierrot' or 'pierrotte', as in 'little Peters' – Peter the Parrot, if you like. This naming of birds was equally common in England, as seen in mag the pie, jack the daw and, of course, the robin. The long, shaggy wigs that later became the fashion were fancied to resemble the plumage of these new avian arrivals and so attracted the name of 'perruque', a term which the English adopted in the form of 'perwyke', which further altered to 'periwig' before the first element was abandoned to leave 'wig'.

It is also worth mentioning that the price of an exotic parrot was then quite exorbitant, as indeed can still be the case, so the traffic in such birds from Africa and the New World was largely in the hands of those who, when not trapping exotic birds, scoured those waters in search of other booty. Thus was cemented the link between pirates and parrots.

PARTRIDGE and PETARD

Both deriving from the Middle French 'peter', to fart, the 'petard' was a medieval mine used to breach castle walls; one can only assume it made an unusual noise on detonation. Unreliable in the extreme and infamous for detonating as soon as its fuse was lit, its flaws lie at the root of 'hoist by your own petard' as coined by those within the stronghold guffawing at the spectacle of the hapless sapper being blown sky-high on his own device.

The 'partridge' does indeed make a whirring and prolonged

fart-like noise with its wings on take-off, and things that 'peter out' are deemed to expire with a fart. Maintaining the explosives connection with 'petard', a man who specialises in blowing safes has long been known as a 'peterman'.

PAVILION and PAPILLON

English acquired both from the French 'papillon', a butterfly, the small dog with its big, dihedral ears thought to resemble the flying insect. Through a mild change in spelling, the 'pavilion', originally 'pavillion', denoted in French the kind of massive tent used by a marquis (whence 'marquee') on hunting trips or on campaign, which, devoid of any side panels, looked like a massive butterfly. It was, if you like, more of a canopy than a tent, that first term deriving from the Greek 'konopeion', a mosquito net; the cognate 'canapé' likewise derived for the base being 'netted over' by a tasty covering. As for the domestic 'butterfly', a term that was at one time thought by to be a spoonerised mash of 'flutterby', this derives somewhat less romantically from the Dutch 'boterschijt', for the buttery colour of its droppings.

PECCADILLO and PICCADILLY

The Latin 'peccare', to sin, was adopted by Spanish as 'pecado', which quickly produced the diminutive 'pecadillo' for a minor sin; this arrived in late-sixteenth-century English as 'peccadillo', just in time for the new craze of ornate lace ruffs and collars known as 'piccadills' or 'pickadills'. Although some say these were named from the Spanish 'picadillo', a *presumed* development from 'picado', punctured or pierced, whence 'picador', but since no one has ever found any trace of 'picadillo' in print, that suggestion is left somewhat at sea.

Far more likely is that the name was built on the newly arrived 'peccadillo' and applied due to the collars being seen as a manifestation of the minor sin of vanity. London's major producer of pickadills in the early seventeenth century was a tailor called Robert Baker, who had several business interests in the area that acquired the name 'Piccadilly' after he built an imposing residence there that was promptly nicknamed Pikadilly Hall or Pickadilly Hall by the locals.

The Latin root 'peccare' also produced one of the most famous puns in English. Sir Charles Napier was sent to Sind in modern Pakistan in 1842 to quell an insurrection; having done so with considerable brutality, he supposedly sent a one-word telegram announcing 'Peccavi', I have sinned (or Sind). In reality he sent no such message.

PECULIAR and PECUNIARY

Both come from the Latin 'pecus', cattle, which explains the opposite meanings of 'peculiar', those of 'unique and personal' and 'strange', in that your own cattle were peculiar, or unique, to you whilst all other cattle were unknown or strange to you as they were peculiar, or unique, to someone else. Cattle were once the main measure of wealth with the Latin 'pecunia', wealth in cattle, producing 'pecuniary'. Your 'capital' was measured by the number of 'head' of cattle you had and 'chattel' is but a variant of 'cattle'. This cow-wealth link can also be seen in the Irish 'tlus', cattle, which moved into Welsh as 'tlws' to mean a jewel or something of value. The importance of cattle to the ancients is further reflected in the first or leading letter of the alphabet; the Phoenician 'aleph', cognate of the Greek 'alpha', actually meant an ox and our own A started out life upside down to represent a cow's head and horns.

'Fee' has travelled a long way from its Proto-Indo-European roots of 'peku', cattle or livestock, arriving in Old English as 'feoh', to denote an amount payable in cattle, with spin-offs including the 'feudal' system and 'feolaga', a partner in the cattle business, whose title survives today as 'fellow'. Although incognate, the Scottish 'spreath', a cattle raid, gave us 'spree'.

PEDAGOGUE and SYNAGOGUE

In Ancient Greece the 'pedagogue' was the slave charged with taking the master's sons to school, staying with them in class and then bringing them home safely. Taking his title from 'paidos', a child, and the element '-agogue' derived from 'agogos', a leader, the pedagogue picked up assorted knowledge to brandish before his peers, to whom he doubtless appeared a trifle 'pedantic'. Given the implied meaning of 'leader of pupils', when the term shifted to Latin as 'pedagogus' it was used of a teacher, a meaning that was handed on to English in the fourteenth century.

With the Greek 'demos' denoting hoi polloi (no 'the': 'hoi' is Greek for 'the') the political 'demagogue' is likewise named for leading the masses; the military leader, or strategos, hopefully came up with the right 'strategy' to fight the battle. 'Sunagogue', a group of people gathered together to be led, was adopted by the Jewish faith in the form of 'synagogue', a building which also had a slave – the shamash, a caretaker-guardian. In early-twentieth-century New York, that title was humorously applied to the house detective of a large hotel before, in the form of 'shamus', broadening to embrace any private detective.

PELL-MELL and MALL-RAT

In 1630 London was hit by the craze of a new game from Italy called 'pell-mell', from 'pallamaglio', ball-and-hammer. Essentially a game of croquet played with attitude, participants charged 'pell-mell' up and down the pitch, whacking their balls, with the most fashionable pell-mell alley being that laid out beside the street that would eventually adopt the name Pall Mall.

Generally known to Londoners as the Mall, its broad aspect made it a popular venue for people to stroll about, window shopping, and this caused 'mall' to attach to any open, airy walkway. It was not until the 1960s that it attached to the enclosed shopping venue, also characterised by broad walkways, and frequented by gangs of kids called 'mall-rats'.

PENGUIN and WENDY

The names of many seabirds are fraught with error as sailors of the leading maritime nations – England, Spain and Portugal – used different words for the same birds or, worse still, a single term for two different species. 'Penguin' was first used of the now-extinct great auk after it was first seen in northern waters by Welsh sailors, in whose language 'pen gwyn' meant 'white head'. When standing on land, the auk was rather penguin-like in profile, so the same name was extended to the penguins proper when they were first spotted in southern waters.

That early Welsh-Cumbric 'pen', meaning 'head', 'headland' or 'hill', is clearly extant in toponyms from the Pennines to Penzance, but things got a bit out of hand at Pendle Hill. Named Pen by the Cumbric speakers of the area, the promontory was quite happy as such until Old English speakers, unaware of the meaning of 'Pen', added 'Hul', their own term for hill. By the time modern English arrived, Penhul had altered to Pendle; unaware that the name already meant Hillhill, people compounded the tautology by adding their own 'Hill'.

It has long been stated as fact that the name Wendy was invented by J. M. Barrie for the Darling girl in his novel *Peter and Wendy* (1911) – *Peter Pan* was the title of a 1904 play. It is further said that Barrie was inspired to coin the name after the daughter of his friend, W. E. Henley, kept calling him her 'fwendie-wendie'. Nice tale but the name is a truncation of Gwendolen, a Welsh name meaning 'white ring', with Wendy first noted, oddly enough, as a boy's name in the 1881 census of England. To be fair, the works of Barrie did popularise the name for girls.

PERFUME and FUNKY

In the temples of both early Greece and early Rome it was the custom to burn fragrant wood or other pleasant-smelling unguents in sacrificial fires to mask the stench of burning flesh for the attendants, a nicety reflected in the swinging of incense burners in churches today. The metal incense burner is called a thurible, a term based on the Greek 'thuein', to sacrifice. Many ancient temple had their own coterie of sacred prostitutes whose earnings supported the pageantry, and to make themselves more alluring to potential clients these girls took to 'freshening up' with the sacrificial unguents, which is why 'perfume' is derived directly from the Latin 'per fumus', through smoke.

After the Latin 'fumigare', to smoke, had travelled through Old French to produce such terms as 'fungier', to give off smoke, early-seventeenth-century English adopted 'funk' to denote a heavy pall of tobacco smoke or any other atmospheric pollution. The parallel meaning of a state of fear or panic, which emerged in the eighteenth century, is not quite clear but it might simply be an allusion to those so beset finding themselves lost in a fog of fear. Either way, both meanings came together in World War I, during which 'funk hole' denoted the dugouts made into the front wall of a trench to create refuge from any advancing 'funk' of gas, or for those fearful of the next barrage.

In the case of 'funky' as descriptive of certain styles of music, this emerged in America in the early 1950s and was likely born of the fact that such music was then played in smoky dives and bars.

PHILISTINE and PALESTINE

Most likely Aegean in origin, the Philistines arrived in what is now called the Gaza Strip in the early twelfth century BC, so they had been there for about 2,000 years before the so-called Children of Israel turned up. Either way, their territory of Philistia, whence our modern Palestine, was a five-city kingdom of considerable sophistication and civilisation – so how did their name come to denote an uncultured grunt?

Town-and-gown conflict was by no means restricted to Germany but in Jena in the late seventeenth century the running battles took on a very dark hue, with violence escalating through 1693 to culminate in the deaths of several students who had incautiously fallen asleep at their table in an inn. Given the circumstances of the students' deaths, the university pastor took as his text for the memorial Judges 16:19–31, which, recounting the capture of Samson, includes the warning for him to awake because 'the Philistine be upon thee'.

The text also makes it clear that it was not Delilah who cut Samson's hair but an unnamed Philistine man, but that is another matter. It was in this way that 'philistine' entered German university slang to denote any uncultured person. The first non-German use was noted in 1847 in France, whence it was picked up by Matthew Arnold, who made such use of the word in a similar context in his highly influential *Culture and Anarchy* (1869) that he guaranteed the term a home in English for good.

PIANO and PLANTAGENET

The Latin adjective 'planus', flat or level, has obvious offspring such as 'plane' and the 'plan' that is laid out, as indeed is an 'explanation', with a 'plaza', 'pizza', and the flatfish 'plaice' all being equally flat. 'Platitudes' smooth things over and the 'platypus' has broad, flat feet but no need of the prefix 'duck-billed' as there is no other kind.

Through the same spelling shift that altered 'plaza' to 'piazza' (whence 'pizza'?), early Italian morphed 'plano' into 'piano' to mean 'flat', 'low' or 'even', and this was adopted by medieval Italian musicians to mean 'soft' or 'low' in terms of volume. When the Italian Bartolomeo Cristofori invented the piano in 1700, he called it the 'piano-e-forte', soft-and-loud, as the instrument could have its volume regulated by pedal-operated dampers.

The botanical 'plant' is put into the ground, which is then pressed flat with the 'plantigrade' foot. The royal household of the later Middle Ages took its name from the 'planta genesta', the common broom plant, with 'Plantagenet' originally the nickname of Geoffrey of Anjou, father of Henry II and founder of the dynasty, who wore a sprig of broom in his helmet as a sign that he would sweep aside all before him.

POMMIE and GRENADE

There are several acronymic explanations put forward for the first term in the heading, usually alleging that transportees to Australia had to wear tunics proclaiming P.O.M.E, Prisoner Of Mother England, P.O.H.M, Prisoner Of His Majesty, or some such. Unfortunately for such fanciful yarns, the term was not recorded until 1913, when Australian old timers interviewed about their youth recalled the term as a street taunt aimed at new arrivals from England in the 1880s: unused to the sun, they were burned red, like pomegranates. Children would follow such newly arrived immigrants chanting, 'Immigranate-Pomegranate', the second term eventually shortening to 'Pomme' or 'Pommie'.

As for the 'grenade', this too took its name from the seedy nature of that same fruit, in allusion to the bits of shrapnel dispersed on detonation. Grenadiers were naturally selected for their height and upper-body strength, with the British Grenadiers made all the more imposing by the tall bearskin hats they first wore after taking them from the French Grenadiers of the Imperial Guard vanquished at Waterloo. The bearskin should not be called a busby as that is a different form of military headgear altogether.

PONTOON and PONTIFF

In the later sixteenth century, 'pontoon', derived from the Latin 'pons', a bridge, described the kind of flat-bottomed boat – hence 'punt' – used by armies to create temporary bridges over rivers. By 1914 'pontoon' had come to describe the military bridge itself, rather than that on which it floated, this also being the time at which British troops fighting in World War I first encountered the French game of vingt-et-un, or twenty-one, which was promptly nicknamed 'French bridge', as in the card-game, in mockery of its simplicity. Having involved the word 'bridge', albeit in reference to the game which was probably named from the Russian 'biritch', whist, the Tommies spun 'French bridge' into 'pontoon' as that was the physical bridge with which they were most familiar.

As the Christians saw their power growing in Rome they smothered or adopted pagan practices and sites, one of their first moves being to drive all the old pagan prophets, or vaticinatores, from the Mons Vaticanus and claim it as their own powerbase. They also hijacked the title of the once-powerful Pontifex, the High Priest of Rome whose epithet meant 'bridge-maker'. This high priest and his entourage of 'pontiffs' were certainly seen as forming a bridge between man and the gods but there is also some suggestion that their office was lumbered with the job and cost of maintaining the actual bridges of the city.

PORK and PORCELAIN

With both deriving from the Latin 'porcus', a pig, the former perhaps needs no explanation, but it is the prurient minds of sixteenth-century sailors we have to thank for 'porcelain'.

Throughout the South Seas and the East, cowry shells were used as wampum and nicknamed 'porcellas' by the sailor-traders who fancied that, when held in the vertical, the shell's opening resembled a sow's vulva; it must have been all those long periods at sea. Anyway, when Portuguese and Dutch traders started bringing a new type of china out of China in the early 1500s, the white, translucent sheen reminded them of the sheen on the inside of the porcellas so they called it 'porcellana'.

POSTHUMOUS and POSTERIOR

'Posthumous' is a corrupt rendition of the Latin 'postumus', the last-born, which denoted a child born after the father's death or a book published after the death of its author. These associations with death and burial prompted English to impose a wholly unnecessary H through the misconception that 'humus', earth, was somehow involved. So in its pure meaning 'post(h)umous' is a kindred term of the 'posterior', the rear or last part of the body, and 'preposterous', which is basically the Latin version of 'cart-before-the-horse' or indeed 'posterior-about-face'.

PRESS GANG and CULPRIT

Both of these owe life to the early French 'prest', to lend or to stand ready.

Operating with full legal backing, the press gangs of old would round up any likely candidates and drag them back to short-crewed ships. Under English law no contract can stand valid until money has changed hands (hence 'finance' from the French 'fin', the close), so each new 'recruit' was offered a shilling's advance and ordered to sign his papers. Any prevarication and the hapless were taken off to meet the boatswain's cat, after which they returned, pen in hand, and with a far more positive approach to their new circumstances.

Most of the press gangs' hunting grounds were off-limits to the army, which had to rely instead on recruiting sergeants, who toured the inns with tales of a glorious life; anxious not to drop quota and thus return to normal duties, these men were not above employing subterfuge to trick the unwary into taking 'the King's Shilling'. It is said that glass-bottomed drinking mugs came into being to allow the cautious to check for any unwanted coins in their beverage, which might otherwise slide into the mouth and so land them in the army.

As for 'culprit', this too is born of the other meaning of 'prest', to stand ready. In seventeenth-century trials and grand jury proceedings the prosecution would rise and, pointing at the defendant, proclaim, 'Culpable; prest d'verrer nostre bille!' – He is guilty and we are ready to prove our indictment. 'Culprit' was born of court recorders abbreviating this to 'Cul. prest' or employing the variant 'prit'. Juries feeling the prosecution had failed to prove their case returned the indictment with 'ignoramus', we take no notice of this, scrawled across it, and peeved prosecutors who thought this an indication of stupidity adopted that term with its modern meaning.

PRESTIGE and STRAIT-JACKET

The Latin 'stringere', to pull hard on a rope or to draw tight, produced cognates such as 'strangle', 'strain', 'stringent' – and the 'astringent' that tightens the skin – as well as the 'constraints' placed upon the unruly and the 'strait-jacket' they go into if constraints fail. It never has been 'straight-jacket', no matter the 'restraint' with which it holds the patient straight and upright; this 'strait' is the same as the Straits of Gibraltar, or any other 'restricted' maritime passage. 'The straight and narrow', as meaning the path trod by the righteous, is also a common error; Matthew 7:14 cautions that: 'Strait is the gate and narrow is the way which leadeth unto life.'

'Strict' and 'stress' are also cognates, with those between whom there is genuine affection experiencing 'distress' if they are forced apart. The Medieval Latin 'districtus' meant the restriction of offenders by the imposition of the law, this morphing to the 'district' under said jurisdiction. Deriving from the Latin expression 'praestringere oculos', to bind the eyes – to blind, in other words – 'prestige' in the sixteenth century denoted deceit, fraud or the kind of illusion created by a magician. Not until the opening of the twentieth century did the term start to acquire overtones of the meaning it holds today.

PUMPERNICKEL and SANTA CLAUS

There are many fanciful suggestions as to how the dark and stodgy German rye bread got its name, most of them likely just diversions to distract sniggering children from the fact that the name is but the German for 'devil-farter', due to the effect it has on those who consume it. The metal 'nickel' was likewise named by German miners, who called it 'Kupfernickel', or devil-copper, because it resembled said metal yet yielded none.

To the Greeks, Poseidon was the lord of the seas and the protector of most afloat – but not all; somewhat bizarrely, the original version of *The Poseidon Adventure* (1911) was being screened on HMRS *Titanic* the night she met her Waterloo. As the glory that had been Ancient Greece was eroded by the encroaching barbarians from the West, the headland temples to Poseidon throughout the Mediterranean, the Aegean and the Near East were either destroyed or turned over to the veneration of the Germanic/Teutonic equivalent, Hold Nickar. Then, with the rise of Christianity, Hold Nickar was demonised as Old Nick and the most closely named saint, Nicholas, shoehorned in as replacement protector of seafarers.

The city of Myra in modern Turkey claimed to hold the skeleton of St Nicholas and did such a roaring trade in the burgeoning pilgrimage business that, in 1087, the Italian port of Bari dispatched a raiding party to nick Nicholas's bones and bring them back, in order to start their own pilgrimage scam. But as well as such bones as the raiders managed to steal during an unseemly struggle over the saint's remains, they also came away with tales of Nicholas's boundless generosity and gifting, particularly towards children. In Dutch, Saint Nicholas is Sinterklaas, whence Santa Claus.

PUNK and SPUNK

Both of these derive from the Gaelic 'spong', tinder or rotten wood, with 'spunk', a spark, noted in Scottish usage in the 1530s; the relevant entry in the *OED* includes a quote from 1646: 'To make white powder . . . the best I know is by the powder of rotten willows [or] spunck.' The 'spunck' referred to is a material otherwise known as amadou, a tinder made from layers of woodland fungus soaked in nitrates. So ancient is this fire-starting method that white amadou and flints were found among the possessions of Ötzi the Iceman, a 5,000-year-old mummified corpse found in 1991 in the Alps.

First noted in such usage in the 1880s, 'spunk' in the UK is now a vulgar synonym for semen, while in the USA it denotes courage or a feisty spirit, an application first noted in the 1770s. The notion of white powder is doubtless responsible for the UK usage, with the connection to spark and fire responsible for the American usage. The cognate 'punk' was also used for tinder or rotten wood, and through associations with that which is of little value, was being used in the late 1500s in the UK for prostitutes, a usage that made the transition to the USA, where, in the early 1900s, the term was being used of passive male homosexuals or male prostitutes. By the 1920s, most sexual overtones were abandoned, leaving 'punk' descriptive of any petty criminal or worthless young male.

Had it not been for the advent of punk rock in America in the early 1970s, the term might have faded entirely from use, but apart from saving 'punk' from its well-earned place on the linguistic scrapheap, the punk movement also gave rise to the misuse of 'Mohican' for the plumed punk hairstyle. That misuse seems to stem from the plethora of films such as *Hawkeye and the Last of the Mohicans* – which, by definition, only has a couple of Mohicans in the story – but such films did feature a large number of the 'baddie' Mohawks who fought with the French and are always shown, again somewhat inaccurately, with their heads shaved into a central plume of hair. The punks just got their Mohawks confused with their Mohicans.

PYGMY and POINT-BLANK

The Latin 'pungere', to prick, has many English descendants; a 'pungent' smell is one that pierces through all others; 'punctuation' pierces or breaks up text; the 'punctilious' observe every minor 'point'; and the Spanish card game 'punto' requires players to make 'points' against the bank with the avid player being a 'punter'. A car tyre can get a 'puncture' and the remote relative 'pounce', now a verb, was previously a noun denoting the pointed and piercing talons of a bird of prey, and 'poignant' thoughts pierce the memory.

Also cognate is the Latin 'pugnus', a fist, hence 'punch', 'pugilism', 'pugnacious' and possibly the 'pug' dog with its punched-in face. 'Expunge' used to mean punching someone's lights out or driving out the occupying force of a garrison, while that which is 'repugnant' is driven away with punches. 'Pugme', the Greek cognate of 'pugnus', gave rise to an ancient unit of measure called the 'pygme', which was set as the length from the elbow to the knuckles of the clenched fist; as such it was similar to the English 'ell', from the bend in the arm to the tip of the middle finger, hence 'elbow'. In the form of 'pygmy', the term was applied not only to the diminutive peoples of Africa but also to any breed of animal smaller than the norm – the pygmy shrew, for example.

In the cognate form of 'point' we find people 'appointed' to serve in office from a specific point in time; if sacked they will feel a sense of 'disappointment'.

'Point-blank', however, comes from archery and the original

French form 'point-blanc', or aim at the white. On a medieval archery butt – hence the 'butt' of a joke – the bullseye was not gold but white, and an archer standing close enough to the target to fire straight at the bull, without any elevation to create trajectory, would have to be standing very close indeed. It was this sense of proximity and directness that caused the expression to shift to a meaning of direct and plain talking – 'I told him point-blank', for example.

Point-blank made the transition to artillery, and in a round-about way is linked to the origins of 'klick' as in 'kilometre'. All ranging starts from the barrel level, or point-blank, with modern pieces elevated by one major ratchet whose fine-tuning between each notch is set by another dial. Each major notch on the ratchet takes the range out another kilometre and does so with a distinctive 'click'; the K spelling arose in Vietnam and likely did so to maintain a connection with 'kilometre'.

PYRRHIC and PYROTECHNICS

The 'pyrrhic' victory, one achieved at such cost that it is hardly a victory at all, celebrates Purrhos, Latinised as Pyrrhus and so named for his flaming red hair, who as king of Epirus in northern Greece secured a bitter victory over the Romans at Asculum in 279 BC. When he was congratulated by the few generals he had left, Pyrrhus wryly opined that another such victory and all would be lost.

The Greek 'pura', a funeral fire, moved into Latin as 'pyra', whence the English 'fire' and the funeral 'pyre', which brings to mind the 'bonfire', originally 'bone-fire'. Cognates include 'pyrotechnics', a fancy name for fireworks, and 'pyrite', otherwise known as fools' gold, which was used by the ancients to strike sparks to start fires.

QUACK and SALVER

The sixteenth-century medical charlatan would leap up on a
bench in the village square – hence 'mountebank' – and 'quack
on' about his 'salves', or life-saving medicines. Thus these
erstwhile snake-oil salesmen were known as 'quacksalvers', but
by the early seventeenth century the second part of the term
had been abandoned – and we still have the 'title' of quack's
assistant. Toads were then roundly believed to be lethally toxic
so, to prove the worth of his medicine, the quack would call
upon his stooge to eat a piece of toad and then 'save his life'
with a dose of his medicine. This 'toad-eat' survives today as the
obsequious 'toady'.

The second element of 'quacksalver' now describes the kind
of silver tray carried by butlers to serve drinks but in the late

sixteenth century, when poisoning the irksome was all the fashion, the rich and powerful needed a food taster. Keenly observed by host and guests alike, all watching for the slightest hint of ill-being, this unfortunate patsy would sample all the food on his salver before it was served; the side table at which he conducted the tasting was called the 'credenza', as this food-tasting gave credence to the safety of the food.

The military 'salvo' is likewise derived from 'safe' or 'save', in that it originally described something akin to a salute, the discharging of weapons being a common gesture indicating the visiting entourage was safe to approach. As for the mechanics of the modern military 'salute' – a simple truncation of 'salutation' – these were born of knights lifting their visors to show their faces in respect and to indicate a lack of intent to engage.

QUARANTINE and QUARTERMASTER

Taking their cue from the countless references to forty days and forty nights in the Bible, early doctors thought a confinement of such a period must have a beneficial effect on the patient. Obviously the Latin 'quadru' and 'quadri', consisting of four, are the foundation of 'quarantine' and countless other terms in modern English usage, such as 'quadruped', 'quadratic' and the 'quart', which is equal to a quarter of a gallon. Less obvious are the 'quarry' from which 'square', or four-cornered, stones are cut; the '(s)quadron' of cavalry or the infantry detachment of 'squaddies' that used to form up on the battlefield in a square, and the 'quire' of paper that is folded in four.

With the military camps of old divided into four sections, 'quarter' came to mean an area set aside for a specific purpose, whether it formed a fourth of the whole for not – hence, for example, the Latin Quarter of Paris, so named in the Middle Ages for its being the haunt of university staff and students who chose to converse in Latin. On a smaller scale, 'quarters' could also denote an individual's living area, hence the title of the quartermaster, whose job it was to sort out lodgings for the troops as well as sourcing and supervising the store of food required to feed them. The average knight of old was usually a pretty well-heeled individual and if captured in battle he were worth more alive than dead, so he would be 'granted quarter', or accommodation, while the ransom details were thrashed out with his family.

Known in the 1600s as 'close fights' and by the eighteenth century 'closed quarters', these were sturdy blockhouses on the decks of merchant or fighting ships, which came into play if a hostile boarding looked inevitable. The defending crew could retire to these structures with enough musket-and-shot to create such a withering crossfire across their own decks that invaders were soon convinced a hasty retreat would be the healthiest option. Close or closed quarters were used only when the enemy was face to face, but when the designation moved ashore it was misunderstood to mean 'close' as in 'near' and not 'close' as in 'shut'.

QUESTION and CONQUEROR

Linked by the Latin 'quaerere', to seek, the 'questioner' seeks answers while the other seeks 'con-quest'; the original 'conqueror' was not a victor but rather one who sought control of a realm or throne, whether victorious or not – he was on a 'quest', if you prefer. The thread continues through the allied 'inquire' and those who seeking to 'acquire' what they 'require'; on securing what they seek, they feel 'exquisite'.

QUICKSAND and COUCH GRASS

From the Old English 'cwic', alive, with overtones of 'fast', 'quick' only arrived in the fifteenth century, when people with a lively mind were described as 'quick-witted'.

'Quicksand', or sand that appears to be alive, is basically very sandy water and thus so buoyant that no one can drown in it, no matter how deep it is. Standard advice is simply to lie down and roll back to terra firma. Originally 'quick grass' and then 'quitch grass', the springy growth was named for its lively bounce, the final corruption occasioned by its use as stuffing by early upholsterers.

The original meaning of 'quick' is still clear in expressions such as 'the quick and the dead' and 'cut to the quick', originally descriptive of a sword blow of sufficient severity to cut through the armour and into the living flesh beneath. The 'quick' is also the living part of the finger or toenail, which can become inflamed by a 'quickflaw', a term that corrupted to 'whitflaw' before becoming the painful 'whitlow'.

QUIM and BUNK

Both terms hark back to the surname of Edward Buncombe, who moved to America from Britain in 1768 upon inheriting a plantation on the shore of the Albemarle Sound, North Carolina. His surname means '(of the) reed' or 'reedy valley', with 'combe' deriving from the Welsh 'cwm', a cleft or valley that, in the form of 'quim', made something of a natural transfer to the vagina in the early eighteenth century.

Ned Buncombe went from strength to strength in the Carolinas, with the local county taking his name, under which it was in 1820 represented in Congress by Felix 'Windbag' Walker. As Congress wrestled with the complex question of the Missouri Compromise – whereby that state could retain its slaves yet still join the Union – Walker rose somewhat unsteadily to his feet and launched himself on the full seas of a rambling speech that had nothing to do with the question under fraught debate. It was late in the day so calls for him to desist were angry and peppered with expletives, but, rising above such verbal onslaught, Walker imperiously waved aside all objections, stating that he was not speaking to Congress but to Buncombe. It may sound apocryphal but the incident is more than sufficiently attested in contemporary records.

In political circles, 'buncombe' was immediately taken up as a synonym for verbal rubbish, this quickly morphing to 'bunkum' and finally 'bunk', with spin-offs including the American police Bunco Squad, which deals with fraud; 'doing a bunk', to slip quietly away when in trouble; and 'bunking off' school on some invented pretext of sickness or family issues.

QUINSY and ANGOSTURA

The Indo-European root of 'angh-', tight or painful, produced in early German 'engen', to pinch, whence 'angst', 'anxious', 'anguish' and 'anger', all emotional conditions that leave you with a sensation of constriction in the chest or a feeling that you are trapped in a tight corner. 'Angina', first noted in late-sixteenth-century English, then meant a tightening of the throat due to infection; 'angina pectoris' emerged in the late 1700s with the somewhat confusing meaning of 'tight throat in the chest'. That same root of 'angh-' originally arrived in Greek as 'ankhein', to strangle, which, put together with 'kuon', dog, produced 'kunankhe', a dog collar. With a secondary meaning of 'sore throat', 'kunankhe' moved into Middle Latin as 'quinancia', thence to Old French as 'quinencie', on to Middle English as 'quinesye', and finally into modern English as 'quinsy'.

The modern Venezuelan city of Ciudad Bolívar was originally named Angostura del Orinoco because it stood at a narrowing, or strangling-point, if you prefer, of that river, and it was here in 1820 that Simón Bolívar's liberation army found itself stalled by an epidemic of Montezuma's revenge and scurvy. The locals showed Bolívar's doctors how to prepare a bitter herbal concoction that got them all back on fighting form, and word spread. 'Angostura bitters' were quickly adopted by the British in India, who were already using quinine waters to combat malaria, this being the birth of the gin and tonic. Angostura bitters were used to produce the medicinal pink gin; because the bitters were swilled round the glass and then discarded before the gin went in, this gave rise to the misconception that the bitters were somehow toxic – they are not.

QUINTAIN and PUNJAB

The Sanskrit 'panca', five, arrived in early Greek as 'pente', and after some fairly torturous alterations, arrived in Latin as 'quinque', whence the French 'cinque'. Known in the UK as Whitsun, or White Sunday, Pentecost is observed on the fiftieth day of the year, while Pentateuch is a term denoting the first five books of the Old Testament. With its five points, the pentagram is generally associated with Satanic practice, but there is no historical evidence of this; the goat's-head pentagram, for example, as featured in gothic devil-horror films, is actually the registered trademark of the San Franciscan Church of Satan (founded 1966), which, in the heady days of Hollywood hedonism, counted as members Sammy Davis Jr, Jayne Mansfield and even Liberace.

In a Roman military camp, the fifth 'street' was wider than the others as this was the area reserved for military training and exercise, hence the 'quintain' tilting target used as practice by knights of old. By distortion of 'quino' we also get the lottery game of 'keno', requiring five winning numbers. Another cognate of the Sanskrit 'panca' is the Old Persian 'panj', whence the 'Punjab', or Land of the Five Rivers, and the refreshing 'punch' which, developed by the British in India, comprised five ingredients: alcohol, sugar, fruit, water and spice.

the shepherd could see which was had received his attentions

R

RADDLED and ROUND ROBIN

The sheep of old got daubed with all sorts: tar was used to disinfect minor injuries, hence 'all tarred with the same brush', while failure to issue such basic care might result in the 'loss of the sheep (not ship) for a ha'porth of tar'. Sometimes creosote was used to much the same purpose, hence its name, which derives from the Greek 'kreas', flesh, and 'soter', saviour. In the mating season the belly of the ram was painted red, or 'raddled', so the shepherd could see which ewes had received his attentions and which not. 'Well raddled' or the even less pleasant 'raddled old bag' came to apply to women thought to be enthusiastic in the horizontal jogging department.

In the early eighteenth century, petitions of grievance were difficult to get started on a man-of-war since the captain, should he deem the petition groundless and vexatious, could exercise his right to hang the first-signed, holding him responsible for inciting unrest or even mutiny. Thus began the ruse of the 'round robin', which presented the signatures in a circle on the document itself or on a strip of ribbon attached thereto; in such manner it was impossible to determine the order of signing. 'Robin' here is a corruption of 'ribbon', which itself originally presented as 'ruban', or red, the traditional colour of ribbon as attested by the 'red tape' that binds the official documents that bind our collective lives today. It was in 1890s America that 'round robin' was first used for a competition in which all contestants had to play against each other, most likely so named as the competitors were imagined to be standing in a circle to face-off each other.

RANDY and RANDOM

From the German 'Rand', a rim, edge or outer limit, sixteenth-century English created 'random' to describe a man or horse running at the outer limit of capability, this term sidestepping to the world of artillery to denote a gun firing at its maximum range. Raised to maximum elevation to achieve such range, all accuracy was lost and the scattered pattern of the shot falling 'at random' caused the term to acquire overtones of haphazardness.

'Randy' behaviour is usually at or beyond the outer limits of social acceptability. Meanwhile the South African rand was so named for its first being struck from gold found in the Witwatersrand, a fifty-six-mile-long mountain ridge near Johannesburg.

RAPE and **RAPTURE**

The Latin 'rapere' meant 'to forcibly remove', with 'rape' devoid of sexual overtones until the nineteenth century, when that became pretty much the only accepted meaning of the term. Although 'rape' had been used in the sexual sense on occasion, dating back to the late sixteenth century, the overwhelming usage had been in the sense of carrying something away as prize or booty, as can be seen in the titles of two works, both of a mock-heroic nature: *The Rape of the Bucket* (1622) by Alessandro Tassoni and *The Rape of the Lock* (of hair), published by Alexander Pope in 1712. The *OED* carries quotes indicating this meaning persisted until quite recently: 'steadily clutching all that he had raped' (1863) and 'The stone walls on either side pressed close, threatening to rape from us our faithful caravan' (1927).

This original meaning of 'rape' is still visible in the 'rapture' that carries one away on a wave of emotion, the 'raptors' that make off with carrion, and the 'rapids' in a river that carry away incautious swimmers.

RASPBERRY and **RIFLE**

The Latin 'erasus', past participle of 'eradere', to scrape away or erase, is responsible for the 'raspberry' with its 'abrasive' cane, the sharp file known as a 'rasp', and talk of 'razing' buildings. 'Razor' and 'rasher' are cognates, as indeed is a 'rash' on the skin and the 'rascal' who, of old, likely had rough or scrofulous skin himself. Early Dutch produced the distant cousin 'riffelen', to rub, scrape or plunder, and the main difference between a 'rifle' and a smooth-bore gun is the helical groove in the barrel of a rifle that scrapes a line in the bullet to impart spin, thus leaving the unique ballistic 'fingerprint' that was first used to identify a UK killer as early as 1835. The 'riffraff' scraped from the workshop floor is cognate, as is the 'raffle' in which one winner gathers up or scrapes away all the winnings.

RECTOR and RECTUM

The Latin 'regalis', royal, has many offspring, ranging from the German 'Reich', the English 'right' or 'recht' and even the Hindi 'raj' and 'maharaja'. When you 'reach' for something you do so in a 'di-rect' or straight line and when the zealous 'overreach' themselves it is a reference to an inexperienced horse trying to run too enthusiastically and injuring its forelegs with its hind hooves.

The cognate element 'reg' crops up in 'regiment', 'regent', 'regal' and 'region', originally a specific part of the country ruled by a warlord appointed by the king. From the altered form of 'rect' we have 'director', 'direction', 'correct', 'rectitude' and the ecclesiastical 'rector', appointed to guide the congregation in the right direction. In Rome, 'rector' first denoted the pilot of a ship who gave instructions to the man at the 'gubernum', or rudder, and in time that 'gubernator' or 'gubinor' took office as the 'governor'. And finally to the 'rectum', which was named for its being that part of the large intestine that finally straightens out for 'direct' exit.

RHUBARB and **BARBARIAN**

Language differences have long been used as a discriminator; the Khoikhoi of the South African Cape speak in a click language intoned on the intake of breath, something trivialised by early Dutch invaders as 'Hottentot', a term inspired by the two most oft-heard syllables, 'hott' and 'tott'. The Asiatic hordes were likewise ridiculed by the Greeks as the 'Ta-ta', intimating baby-like speech, but after the Greeks found out how these people liked to party this was modified to 'Tartar' as inspired by Tartarus, a hell even deeper than Hades. And, for the Romans, any non-Latin speaker was a linguistically incompetent dolt dismissed as a 'Ba-ba', which extending into 'Barbarian' and also gave a name to the Berbers and the Barbary Coast, the occupants of which were originally called the 'Barberi' or just the 'Beri', a possibly origin of the otherwise obscure 'as brown as a berry'.

And so to 'rhubarb'. As far as the later Europeans were concerned, the Barbarians lived in the East, as it was from here that hailed the likes of Genghis Khan and Attila the Hun, who, far from Germanic in origin, was of Asiatic descent and the leader of a rabble of troublesome nomads booted out of Northern China to drift west, bringing the bitter plant with them.[2] By the tenth century the plant was proliferating wild along the banks of the

---

2 The confusion between the Chinese Huns and the Germans arose during the 1899 Boxer Rebellion in China. His ambassador having been chopped up in the street, Kaiser Wilhelm II dispatched his troops to Peking ordering them to grant no quarter but to behave like the Huns under Attila. His speech was pilloried in cartoons showing the Asiatic and spiky-hatted Huns morphing into German troops, who themselves then wore spiked helmets, and Huns became a new nickname for the Germans.

Volga, previously known as the Rhu or the Rha, and as that river served as the vector to ship the plant ever westwards as its name shortened from 'rhubarbarian' to 'rhubarb'.

America remained rhubarb-resistant until the 1820s but it would be there, on the Californian movie sets, that the plant would acquire its additional meaning of 'verbal rubbish'. In scenes calling for crowds of extras looking mean and threatening, actors were directed to repeat the word over and over so that, on camera, their facial movements made them look suitably angry.

RIVER and RIVALS

Rivers and streams often formed natural boundaries between warring factions, so from the Latin 'rivus', a brook or stream, we derive both of the above. With water transport once the main method of long-distance travel, small boats would carry passengers to the 'riverbank', where they were said to 'ad rive' or 'arrive'. The use of 'rive' for riverbank is clear in French denominations such as 'Rive Gauche', the Left Bank of the Seine in Paris, and its expanded use to denote the seashore, hence the fashionable 'Riviera'.

A classic case of river-rivalry was that of two American tribes, the Houmas and the Bayougoula of Louisiana, who fought over fishing and hunting rights on the banks of the Mississippi. In 1700, demarcation was settled and a totem stick smeared with blood was driven into the bank at the agreed point, with the city now standing there called Baton Rouge.

ROAM and ROMANCE

Pilgrimage was the tourism of its day, with the domestic 'biggie' being the shrine of Thomas Beckett at Canterbury. Pilgrims were recognisable by their heavy-duty capes made from a cloth called 'gaverdine', the Middle French for a pilgrim and a term surviving today as 'gabardine'. The easy pace set by mounted pilgrims from nearby London was known as the Canterbury trot, this now surviving as 'canter'. But serious pilgrims had Rome in their sites.

Having decided to embark on such a quest, the natural desire was to take in as many other sites en route to the city, so it is not impossible that 'roam' is a variant of 'Rome'. It must here be said that many sources, including the *OED*, regard this suggestion with scepticism, but as all those sources, including the *OED*, are in agreement that the true origin of 'roam' is unknown, it must remain a valid contender; Professor Skeat, the pre-eminent nineteenth-century etymologist, certainly accepted it.

With a few notable exceptions, seventeenth-century English writers were a trifle staid and tended not to indulge in gushy sentiment or tales of wild love-affairs and frivolous adventure so, any wanting a bit of spice in their reading, had to turn to French and Italian novels which were written in 'romantic' languages, or those that were Latin-based.

S

SABOTAGE and SAVATE

Both terms are French in their origin and both are descendants from 'sabot', a clog.

A rather brutal form of kickboxing, 'savate' developed in the criminal subculture of early-nineteenth-century Marseille, where the word was a regional variant of 'sabot'; basically the 'savateurs' would kick the living daylights out of each other with wooden clogs. Deaths were common, as one might imagine.

As for 'sabotage', this was born in northern France at about the same time as those in the south were perfecting their homicidal clog skills. The term first applied to work carried out by unskilled, clog-shod labourers to such a poor standard as to raise suspicions of malicious intent. The term lurched closer to its modern application during the French rail strike of 1912, when disaffected workers cut the rail ties, also called sabots, to derail trains driven by scab labour. The term entered English as a result of the military presence in France during World War I.

It should perhaps be said that clog fighting was not unknown in northern England but, unlike the savateurs, participants were bound by rules requiring them to keep their hands behind their backs and kick only below the knee. Prancing around in such a manner the combatants looked like a pair of country dancers, so 'shindig' was also used of a party or local hop, while clog fighting was also known as 'purring'.

SAD and SATIRE

The precursor of 'sad' was the Old English 'saed', which in turn had been built on the Latin 'satiare', to provide with enough, whence also 'sate', 'satiate' and 'satisfy'. Not until the fourteenth century did 'sad' acquire connotations of emotional state; prior to this the term denoted people slumped at the dining table having eaten more than was good for them.

Popular with Roman gluttons was the 'satura lanx', which basically translates as a meal served on a massive plate, or 'lanx', and which can sate any appetite. (The Roman 'bilanx', weighing scales comprising two large pans, entered English as 'balance'.) A composite dish of diced meats, fruits and vegetables, 'satura lanx' was commonly abbreviated to 'satira', with this form of the name also applied to entertainments presenting mixed acts, usually of a bawdy or 'satirical' nature. When this last term first appeared in English at the start of the sixteenth century it presented as 'satyre', retaining that form until the mid-eighteenth century through the mistaken notion that the bawdy and raucous Satyrs of Greek mythology were somehow involved. There certainly were bawdy burlesques that the Ancient Greeks called 'Satyr plays', but these had nothing to do with the evolution of 'satire'.

SALARY and SALAMI

The widespread notion that salt was so expensive it was used to pay the Roman legionnaires is based on the mid-First Century writings of Pliny the Elder who, in his *Natural History* xxi:41, asserts: 'the (Roman) soldier's pay was originally salt and the word "salary" derives from it'. But Pliny, it must be remembered, also wrote at great length on how to render a knife capable of chopping up diamonds by soaking the blade in goat's blood, so reliability is not his long suit. Yet upon this very shaky foundation is built the mighty edifice of the broad assertion that 'salary' is indeed derived from 'sal'. Perhaps so, but not because anyone was actually paid in salt; let us look at some known facts.

If salt was indeed so valuable that Roman soldiers would accept it as pay, why not just stay home and boil seawater to make a killing? If you have seawater and sunshine, as did the Romans in abundance, just let one evaporate the other, as indeed the Romans did. All available records show that, far from being exorbitantly expensive, salt was, pound-for-pound, consistently the same price as grain and other staples. The pay-grades of the Roman soldier are well documented and nary a mention of salt or of any monetary allocation for the purchase of same. In the first century BC the Roman squaddie's basic pay was 225 dinarii, this climbing to 5,000 dinarii by the second century AD.

Never enough to live on, the soldier's basic had to be augmented by substantial annual and quarterly bonuses, called annona and donatives, with the only mentions of edible-issue being allocations of wheat and grain – no salt. At the point when the soldier's total pay was 15,400 denarii per annum only 1,800 denarii of that was the basic and it has been suggested that the soldiers called this the salarium as it was barely enough to keep them in salt; it was, if you like, the Roman soldiers' equivalent of present reference to low pay as 'peanuts'.

The 'salad' is best served with added salt and the 'salami' and 'salsa' are both made with plenty of it. Through spelling changes inflicted by German and French we get 'souse', 'sausage' and 'sauce', which was originally brought to the table in a cup with a small spillage dish, the 'saucer', beneath it. By the end of the seventeenth century the saucer was more often seen beneath a teacup to serve much the same purpose. The flying variety took its name from the 1947 (alleged) sighting of nine UFOs over America's Mount Rainier by Kenneth Arnold, a pilot who described them to be flat discs, like saucers.

True or not, the press coverage spawned the manufacture of plastic flying discs called Frisbees after the Frisbee Pie Company, whose empty dishes had already enjoyed such usage on college campuses for years.

SARCOPHAGUS and SARCASTIC

Deriving from the Greek 'sarx', flesh, the former was linked to the Greek 'phagein', to eat, since it was believed that a limestone sarcophagus would devour the corpse within the fabled forty days. As for the second term, oft dismissed as the lowest form of wit, this took its name from the wounding sneers and insults, metaphorically at least, biting into the listener's flesh, as indeed does the unpleasant 'sarcoma'.

SARDINE and SARDONIC

There is no such fish as a 'sardine'; a sardine is anything that comes out of a tin proclaiming such content. In reality sardines can be the kind of small herring or pilchard that the fifteenth-century English started to harvest off the coast of Sardinia, where such small fry proliferated. Also found on Sardinia is the 'herba sardonia', which is mildly toxic and so incredibly bitter that it induces facial contortions and giving its victims the appearance of bearing a hideous or 'sardonic' grin.

SAXON and SAXOPHONE

The Angles hailed from the hooked or angle-shaped German province now called Schleswig and came over here to establish 'Angleland', which finally softened to 'England' – but still with areas called North and East Anglia. The Saxons who joined them were from the North German Plain and named for their favourite weapon, the 'seax', or long knife. Although made infamous by Hitler in 1934, the original Night of the Long Knives was the fifth-century slaughter on Salisbury Plain of native British chieftains by Saxon mercenaries; Hitler liked the sound of that and so used it for his own party purge.

The 'saxophone' was invented in 1840 by instrument-maker Adolphe Sax, a Saxon by heritage and name.

SCHIZOPHRENIC and SKID ROW

The ultimate root of these is the Greek 'skhizein' (Latin 'scindere'), to split or cleave. From the Latin cognate we get terms such as 'shed', in the sense of 'divest', and 'watershed', sometimes thought to denote a storage unit, but which does in fact refer to a ridge of land that causes the rainfall to divide, or shed, in one direction rather than another – and by extension is a time marker in television schedules after which content of a more adult nature is allowed. From the original root of 'skhizein' there emerged in Greek 'skhide', a piece of wood split from a log, this entering Latin as 'scida', to describe first a thin plate of wood for writing and later the 'sheet' of paper that replaced the wood. The diminutive 'schedula', ideal for jotting down dates and times, entered English as 'schedule'.

Returning to the Greek 'skhizein', this produced not only 'schism' but also 'schizophrenic', which, with its literal meaning of 'split mind', has been responsible for the major misconception that those within the grasp of schizophrenia have a split personality or multiple personalities. Leaving aside any debate as to whether dual personality actually exists or is just an upmarket version of 'It wasn't me, Miss, wot done it; it was Johnny', the term actually refers to a split or division in the mind's functions. The condition is actually marked by a firm adherence to irrational beliefs and the hearing of voices. In the old days that was the first step to sainthood; today it gets you sectioned.

'Skhide' cropped up in Old Norse as 'skith' with much the same meaning, a plank, hence the diminutive 'ski' for snow runners. 'Skate' and 'skid' are cognates of 'ski', with the notion of 'Skid Row' or 'Skid Road' starting in the logging camps of nineteenth-century Canada. This was the nickname of the greased chute down which logs were shot to the river, or of the 'corduroy road' of greased logs along which logs were dragged to the water. Either way this was dirty and low-paid work to which no lumberjack would stoop, so it was usually carried out by drunks or drifters. Tree-jacking was dangerous work so alcohol was banned in the camps, and the jacks had to go 'on the (water) wagon' until they hit town, where they would refer to any area frequented by down-and-outs as Skid Row/Road. Seattle's Pioneer Square neighbourhood was the first district to be so named, in 1865.

SHIT and SHUTTLECOCK

'Acronym' made its first appearance in print in 1943 and words are only invented when there is something new for them to describe. Thus the trend for jargonistic acronyms is new enough to give the lie to the oft-trotted-out yarn that 'shit' is an acronym of 'Store High In Transit', supposedly stipulated for cargoes of manure in ships that might otherwise fill up with methane gas and explode. Besides, apart from high-value guano that gives off no gas at all, who ever transported manure in bulk anyway? 'Fuck' is not an acronym of 'For Unlawful Carnal Knowledge' but derived, not entirely unaided, from the German 'ficken', to strike or 'fidget' about; 'posh' is not an acronym of 'Port Out, Starboard Home', and 'camp' is not an acronym of 'Consorting As Male Prostitute'. It comes instead from the nineteenth-century French stage instruction 'Se camper sur un pied', which essentially told an actor to place all his weight on one leg, bend the other leg and hold out one arm in a decidedly 'camp' posture. But on to 'shit' and 'shuttlecock'.

The German 'schiessen', to shoot, cast off or eject, is responsible for 'shit', as it is indeed for the German equivalent, 'Scheisse'; a 'shyster' is the kind of person, especially a lawyer, considered a metaphorical shit by one and all. The contemporary 'gobshite' has replaced the previous 'blatherskite', which meant pretty much the same thing. Also cognate to 'shit' is 'skot', a tax or a contribution thrown into the pot, hence getting away 'skot-free'. At sea, 'sheet' denotes a rope attached to the foot of a sail to prevent it 'shooting' away; if slackened off to such extent that it exercises no control, a sheet is said to be 'in the wind'. If all 'three sheets (are) in the wind' then the sail is 'footloose and fancy-free', leaving the vessel to lurch about drunkenly in the water.

Also cognate are terms such as the 'skittles' that shoot about when hit in play, 'scooter' and the weavers' 'shuttle' that shoots to and fro as it weaves together the warp and the weft. Not unlike the Japanese game of hanetsuki and others of similar antiquity, the game of battledore and shuttlecork (sic) developed in the British garrison at Poona in India sometime in the 1850s. 'Battledore', to beat, denoted the racket, so it is itself cognate with 'battle', 'batter' (in the physical and culinary senses), 'combat', 'debate' and the 'battery' of artillery that pounds the enemy; in the electrical sense the 'battery' was so named for its series of linked cells discharging in unison, just like an array of artillery. As the feathers on the 'shuttlecork' became more elaborate and colourful, that term morphed into 'shuttlecock' in reference to the cockerel's tail feathers used in its production. In the late 1850s the Duke of Beaufort hosted an informal tournament of the game at his Badminton House estate, and thereby changed the name of the game forever.

SNOB and NOBLE

The two are most certainly linked but the threads that bind them are hard to trace.

The original and prime meaning of 'snob' is the very antithesis of its presently accepted meaning, one who looks down on those perceived as socially inferior. To quote the *OED*, a snob is 'a person belonging to the ordinary or lower classes of society; one having no pretensions to rank or nobility'. Although 'snob' certainly appears to have been born of the Latin 'sine nobilitate', without nobility, how this happened is anything but clear.

There are frequently cited but unsubstantiated accounts of enrolment procedures at both Oxford and Cambridge universities in the early eighteenth century that required the new students to enter their rank in the final column, those having none having to enter 's.nob' as an abbreviation of the above-mentioned Latin phrase. If they ever existed, all such records are long gone, but it has to be said that it was most certainly within Oxbridge slang that 'snob' arose; it is first noted in 1796 as a term for any traders or outsiders who entered the colleges, trying to mix with their betters to sell a few wares or earn a penny or two by running errands for the idle rich. It is worth mentioning that it was these same commoners who ran errands that first attracted 'cad' as a truncation of 'caddie'.

'Snob' is first spotted outside the walls of academe in 1781, as a humorous term for a cobbler, because a man stooped to his last spends his working life looking up to his clients. While the order of those dates appears to present an anachronistic anomaly it does in fact serve to bolster claims of an Oxbridge origin, in that insular use of the term within the colleges would be later noted than any external and general use.

Until the end of the nineteenth century, 'snob' was still understood to indicate a person 'lacking good breeding and good taste' who 'vulgarly admires those of superior rank or wealth' (*OED*), but general use was already starting to invert the meaning to that of a self-obsessed elitist who despised those of lower station. The first time it appeared in print with such meaning was in Shaw's *Getting Married* (1908), in which the author talks of a female character becoming 'an ethical snob of the first water'. Interestingly enough, in Australia 'snob' is still used in something akin to its original sense, in that the 'last' sheep to be shorn is known as the snob in punning reference to the cobbler at his last.

SNOOKER and SNOOK

A variant of terms such as 'snoot', 'snot' and 'snout', 'snook' has enjoyed long service in English as a term for the nose, with the derisive thumbing up of the nose with the open hand known as 'cocking a snook'. And so to India.

In the summer of 1875, General Sir Neville Chamberlain, forebear of the man hoodwinked by Hitler, was stationed in Jabalpur and growing tired of the routine playing of billiards in the mess. Drawing on the other popular game of pyramids, Chamberlain incorporated the coloured balls from that game and 'invented' a new but as yet unnamed game. As the officers tried their hand at this new game, many missed shots and miscued, only to bring humorous taunts from their peers, who hooted and shouted 'Snooker!', then the military slang for a newly drafted cadet, considered by old hands to be a snot-nosed know-nothing.

Despite the apocryphal-sounding nature of this explanation it does appear to be the truth, as investigated and validated by the author Sir Compton Mackenzie in a letter sent in 1939 to *The Billiard Player* magazine. The events at Jabalpur are also detailed under Chamberlain's entry in the *Oxford Dictionary of National Biography*.

SPOUSE and SPONDULICKS

In Ancient Greece contracts and promises of marriage were sealed by the exchange of sacred drinks, and from the Greek 'spendein' or 'spondein', to pour forth a libation, we derive several terms.

The 'sponsor' would pour first, leaving the other party to 'respond' in acknowledgement of the terms of the agreement, which, if related to a marriage, made each the 'spouse' of the other. Naturally, these were solemn occasions with all involved sounding suitably serious, or 'despondent' if one party was promising to give up someone or something they loved, as the terms and conditions were read out in a particular metre of verse still called 'spondee'.

It seems likely that the drinks were measured out or even drunk from a medium-sized cupped shell that became known as the 'spondulos', which later served as wampum in Aegean trade and brings us to 'spondulicks'. Despite the term's associations with British characters of the Bertie Wooster type, it was in American university slang that this first saw light, but whether in reference to the monetary value of the shell or a glib reference to that which 'poured forth' from indulgent relatives is unclear. Either way, when stacked as money those Ancient Greeks thought the shells resembled the vertebrae in the spine, or 'spondyle', with 'spondylitis' the painful condition afflicting the spine.

STOOGE and TWEEZERS

The Latin 'studere', to apply oneself to the acquisition of knowledge, produced 'student', which, by the same corruption whereby 'media' becomes 'meedja', was assimilated into early-twentieth-century American vaudeville slang as 'stoogent' or similar, before arriving at 'stooge', to denote the comedian's trainee who had to act as the 'second banana' or fall guy.

'Studere' could also hold in Latin a meaning of 'to take care of or pay attention to something', and it was this application of the term that arrived in Old French as 'estuier', to guard or shut away, with 'estui' meaning a prison or container. Modern French abandoned the sense of 'prison' but kept 'estui' in the altered form of 'etui' to denote a small case or box, especially one carried by a lady to keep handy small grooming tools such as hair grips and small pincers for plucking unwanted hairs from the face. 'Etui' entered seventeenth-century English as 'etwee' to describe much the same beauty box, with the pincers promptly being promptly renamed 'tweezers'.

SURPLICE and PILLION

With the fatal finger of witchcraft all too swiftly pointed, the churches of old were packed with people anxious to deflect such accusation. There was no proper seating for the common herd so in summer the press could be unbearable for the weak, who had to 'go to the wall' where it was cooler and there were stone ledges to sit on. In the winter it was as cold as charity so the priests, unwilling to share in the privations of their flocks, wore big furry coats to ward off the cold. Realising this smacked of the paganism it was still confronting, the Church invented the 'surplice', from the Latin 'super', over, and 'pellicia', a fur robe.

The ultimate root is the Latin 'pellis', an animal hide, which the hunter would 'peel' from the carcass; 'pillage', by extension, denotes the stripping of a town of its wealth. Also cognate are 'caterpillar', or hairy cat, the 'pile' of a carpet, 'plush' as originally descriptive of a hide with plenty of fur, and the 'pellagra' that attacks the skin. In Roman times animal hair was used to stuff leather balls, so from 'pila', a ball, we get 'pellet', the medical 'pill', the game of 'pilota', now 'pelota', and, through the sense of a gathering together into a clump, the military 'platoon'. The first to ride 'pillion' were servants who sat on the horse's hide behind the master's saddle, and through the well-established shift from P to F we also get 'film', as in a thin covering of hide.

SWASTIKA and ESSENCE

Otherwise known in English as the fylfot for its early use in filling in the bottom sections of stained-glass windows, the 'swastika' has cropped up in cultures ranging from the Amerindian to the Ancient Hebrew. Its name, meaning 'well-being', derives from the Sanskrit 'svasti', in which 'sv' means 'well' and 'asti' means 'being'. The suffix 'ka' is the same as noted in Russian as an affectionate or diminutive addition in words such as 'vodka', little water, and 'babushka', little old lady and, by extension, the kind of headscarf such women wear in Russia.

Interestingly enough, demented Hitler fangirl Unity Mitford was conceived in the Ontario township of Swastika while her equally demented family was there for a spot of gold-mining.

After Hitler's hijacking of the swastika into eternal darkness, the town was invited to change its name to Winston but stuck to its guns, with the polite mayoral rejection of that proposal taking the form of 'Fuck Hitler; we were using the name first.'

The second element of 'asti' formed the Proto-Indo-European root of the Latin 'esse', to be, as crops up in 'essence' and 'quintessential', that pertaining to the fifth essence or element and therefore of prime importance. The Middle English 'interess', denoting things of importance, presented its past participle as 'interess'd', this later altering to 'interest'. Either way, as explained under INTERNECINE, 'inter' does not always have to mean 'between'; sometimes it appears as an intensifier. Also cognate with 'essence' and therefore with 'swastika' are 'presence', 'absence' and, albeit remotely, the toast of 'Prost', or 'well-being'.

SYCOPHANT and PHANTOM

These, and the other terms discussed below, all owe their existence to the Greek 'phainein', to show.

Its first element taken from the Greek 'sykon', a fig, it used to be said that 'sycophant' was born in Ancient Greece to denote an obsequious creep who tried to ingratiate himself with the authorities by denouncing those engaged in the illicit traffic of figs, then considered sacred and a national treasure. There is no evidence to suggest any such embargo existed and the *OED* makes a point of stating that such derivation cannot be substantiated.

Far more likely an origin is the showing of the 'fig', a vulgar and derisory gesture made by thrusting the thumb out between the first two fingers of the clenched fist. Known as the 'fico', this was and is basically synonymous with 'go fuck yourself'; it is still popular throughout modern Italy and Greece and those declaring indifference by saying they 'couldn't give two figs' can only get away with such announcement in company ignorant of the true meaning. Politicians of Ancient Greece trying to stir up the mob against opponents often invited their audience to make such a gesture in derision of that target, and it is likely that 'sycophants' or 'fig-showers' became a term applied to those of little substance who could be goaded in this direction or that as required. 'Sycamore' first attached to a species of fig tree; when the term entered English to describe a kind of maple it carried the prefix 'false'.

The 'phantom' is an apparition that shows itself to those inclined to see such apparitions; 'diaphanous' material allows the corporal delights of the wearer to show through the fabric, as indeed did 'tiffany', which, before becoming a popular girl's name, also described such fabrics. 'Epiphany' first applied to the showing of the infant Christ to the Magi, but can now describe the sudden solving of a long-pondered problem as the answer reveals itself.

SYMPOSIUM and POISON

The former is the Latin transliteration of the Greek 'sumposion', which now denotes a lofty and academic meeting of minds directed at a specific subject, but then denoted what the inefficient are said to be unable to organise in a brewery. Meaning 'to drink together', a 'symposium' or 'sumposion' was a stag party held in the andron, or male-only quarters of the house, to celebrate athletic or hunting victories; all such events were marked by drunkenness and frequently by younger males being initiated into what might politely be euphemised as Athenian practices. Attendees often drank from amethyst cups, believing these to afford a defence against drunkenness, the stone's name deriving from the Greek 'amethustos', not to get drunk, with the 'meth' element allied to terms such as 'methanol' and 'methylene'.

As can be seen in the last element of 'sumposion', toxic substances were then only available in liquid form, and from the Latin cognate 'potare', to drink, we get 'potion'; otherwise known as 'cupid's bow', the groove in the top lip is called the 'philtrum', the Latin for a love potion. The drinking 'pot' is an obvious cognate, with the Irish moonshine called 'poteen' a direct relative too. 'Potassium' was first extracted from 'potash', wood ash soaked in a water pot.

TABLOID and TAVERN

The Latin 'tabula' is a plank or a board to write on, and a few of these nailed together make a 'table'. Apothecaries of the late sixteenth century adopted the French 'tablette', a short plank, for the tablets they made for their patients and the term was not ill-fitting: tablets of the day could choke a horse. Until the 1880s most patients sensibly opted to take their medicines in powder form but in 1884 the pharmaceutical company Burroughs-Wellcome perfected the concentration and compression techniques required to produce a tablet small enough to swallow in comfort, and registered the trade name 'Tabloid'.

The 'oid' suffix was chosen to impart the meaning of 'looking like a tablet' (but not actually being one as previously known). Although people use 'factoid' to mean a compressed snippet of true information, the term, coined by Norman Mailer and backed up by the *OED*, denotes a lie, material presented in the press as truth when it is in fact false. Anyway, the Tabloid range was so successful that anything of diminished size attracted the tag 'tabloid', but the first newspaper to use the term in its masthead, *The Westminster Gazette* of 1 January 1901, was successfully sued by Burroughs-Wellcome.

But the widespread hijacking of 'tabloid' was unstoppable and in 1903 the company was again in court against Thompson & Capper, a still-extant Manchester pharmaceutical firm that was then making free with the term. But for Burroughs-Wellcome this action proved to be something of a pyrrhic victory when the judge ruled that, while they had control over use of the term in any pharmaceutical context, they could not protect it in other spheres as it had already fallen into the public domain. The floodgates were opened: Sopwith produced a compact biplane called the Tabloid; *Punch* and *Tatler* immediately started using the term of their publications, and short plays, for example, were advertised as tabloid tableaux, a fine alliterative tautology if ever there was one.

Going back to Latin, 'taburna' meant a hut or temporary shelter, as might be built from planks, or 'tabula', whence 'tabernacle' and, through a mild spelling change, 'tavern'.

TANTALISE and TANTALUS

The eponymous character behind both terms was Tantalos or Tantalus of Greek mythology, who so upset the gods that he was cast down into Tartarus, a hell set even deeper than Hades' playground. There he had to stand in a lake of cool water with overhanging fruit trees. Beset by eternal hunger and thirst, he reached up for the fruit but the branches pulled back from his grasp; each time he stooped to drink, the water receded, hence 'tantalise' for teasing someone with the unattainable. The lockable decanter frame took its name from the fact that, while you can see the liquids contained therein, you cannot get at them.

TARANTULA and TARANTELLA

Both words celebrate the city and province of Taranto in southern Italy, which in medieval times was so infamous for its indigenous wolf spider that 'tarantula' became a blanket name for all nine hundred species of hairy arachnids. Across the sixteenth and seventeenth centuries, Taranto also became famous for its denizens being taken by fits of frenzied dancing and hysterical rantings, which were branded 'tarantism'.

The dancers were at first said to be victims of the spider's bite but no arachnid venom can induce such symptoms; as with all other hairy arachnids, the bite of the Taranto wolf spider is non-fatal and in fact no more painful that a bee sting. More likely a cause was ergot poisoning through the eating of bread made from diseased rye. Ergot poisoning, similar to a massive dose of LSD, was common throughout early Europe and produced elsewhere similar cavortings – but it was the peasants of Taranto who realised there was a fast buck to be made from the tourist trade.

Applying a spin of religious fever to the incidents, the locals always managed to put on a good show for those who came to see the fun, and their street performances became so famous that composers trotted out frantic pieces ranging from 6/8 time to a frenzied 18/8 time to accompany dancers who leapt about, screaming and banging their tambourines the while, in acts that became known as 'tarantellas'.

TARTAN and STEAK TARTARE

People used to believe that the Tatar nomads put slices of raw meat under their saddles before they rode off in the mornings, so it could tenderise for the evening meal at their next stop, where they'd eat it raw, nicely marinated in horse sweat. Actually this was not quite correct: they *did* sometimes put raw meat under the saddle but only to ease the pain of any saddle sores the horse might have acquired. Be that as it may, French chefs of the early twentieth century, believing the myth, created the raw-meat dish of 'steak tartare', topped with a raw egg and a caper sauce that, as 'tartare sauce', is now more commonly served with fish.

Given the manner in which Genghis Khan and his Tatars liked to party, the spelling altered to 'Tartar', partly through association with Tartarus, a mythological hell even grimmer than Hades, and partly for their hailing from Tartary in Central Asia, whence also the first imports of woven 'tartan' in the late fifteenth century.

Despite the link with Scotland, it should here be said that no clan ever had a unique tartan – everyone wore whatever pattern they fancied. After the Battle of Culloden (1746), in which more Scots fought on the English side than were in the entire

Scottish army, the Act of Proscription banned the wearing of any Highland garb, so the weaving sheds were abandoned and such pattern sticks that did exist rotted where they lay. Then, in 1822, George IV announced a royal visit to Edinburgh and expressed a wish to see all his subjects in their clan tartans, this prompting a rush for kilts in 'traditional' tartans, all invented in a hurry.

TATTOO and TAMPON

The body-art 'tattoo' was a trend first acquired by Captain Cook's crew on their 1764 visit to Haiti and derives from the Haitian 'tatu', a stain, with the first of Cook's crew to be so decorated being the appositely named Robert Stainsby; the military 'tattoo' is wholly separate.

During the Thirty Years' War (1618–48), much of which was fought across Belgium and the Netherlands, the Dutch garrisons dispatched a drum squad at 9.30 p.m. to march through the streets, beating out a distinctive rhythm, to tell the innkeepers it was time to shut the beer taps and for all troops to return to quarters. Known in full as 'doe den tap toe', Dutch for 'turn off the tap', the British army adopted both the practice and the term in the form of 'tattoo'. After any military parade the tattoo squad would signal the end of proceedings, and so popular was the drum squad that by the 1870s their performance had evolved into a pageant of its own. Dutch influence into the United States produced the mournful 'Taps', as played in barracks at close of day or at military funerals.

Long before 'tap' came to mean any kind of on/off flow device, the term denoted a tapered wooden bung used to close off any hole, and, staying with the military, 'tampon' began life in Early French to denote the large cork or wooden plugs fitted to the muzzles of cannon to keep out rain or grit – but the sanitary tampon has martial origins too. During World War I, Kimberly-Clark made field dressings and disposable gas mask filters but was left with stockpiles when the war ended. Remembering the letters of thanks from frontline nurses who used the field dressings as external or internal sanitary wear, they launched them as Kotex pads and put the gas mask filters into boxes branded Kleenex. The internally-worn sanitary devices had to wait a while until the company could come up with a suitably delicate advertising campaign to accompany the launch.

And things have gone full cycle: many soldiers in combat zones today carry a couple of tampons as they make ideal instant plugs for bullet wounds, with a handy cord for medics to remove them on evacuation from the field.

TEDDY BEAR and WARDROBE

In November 1902, President 'Teddy' Roosevelt accepted an invitation from the state governor of Mississippi to go bear-hunting. All the other guests managed a kill but hunting-mad Roosevelt had drawn a blank, so, wishing to please his guest of honour, Governor Andrew H. Longino ordered a captive bear be clubbed into unconsciousness and tied to a tree for Roosevelt to shoot. Not surprisingly, Longino's gesture backfired on him big time: Roosevelt was disgusted and refused to have any part in the charade, leaving the state immediately. The press went into hyper-drive and countless cartoon depictions of the event prompted toymakers to come up with the goods.

'Teddy' is of course a pet form of 'Edward', a name that means 'guardian or warden of the treasures'. Back in the days when a king's clothes cost his weight in gold his outfits were locked in the 'garde-robe' or 'ward-robe' for safety. The 'wardroom' on a warship was once the room in which was stored captured treasure.

TEMPLE and TEMPLATE

The Greek 'temnein', to cut out or set aside, is responsible for these terms, the first of which originally denoted the section of sky 'cut out' by the outstretched hand of the ancient auger determined to 'read' the passage of birds in divination as they passed. When purpose-built places of divination were created, 'temple' simply transferred. The dents on either side of the skull are faithful to the original Greek term, as indeed is the 'template' used as a design to mark the area to be cut out.

TESTICLES and TESTIFY

Before going any further it should be said that while all agree that these terms are linked by the Latin 'testis', a witness, not all agree with the following; perhaps some of those opposed to the following are unaware of the biblical backing accorded the link, as explained under GENUINE.

The gripping of one's own testicles while swearing an oath was common throughout many early cultures, as was the gripping of the testicles of the man to whom a promise was being made. When bearing witness in a Roman court there is strong suggestion that those giving 'testimony' were required to so grip themselves to swear by their manhood that they would tell the truth. Those found guilty of perjury were certainly castrated and hurled to their deaths from the Tarpeian Rock. Draconian, perhaps, but the list of repeat offenders for perjury in Roman courts was extremely short.

THUG and THATCHER

An etymological pairing that will doubtless please those on the left of the political spectrum, both hark back to the Latin 'tegere', to cover or protect, and 'texere', to weave. Thus the terms are close relatives of 'textile', 'context', pretext', 'protect', and the 'detective' who uncovers the facts of a case; also related are 'tile', 'subtle' (previously 'subtile', a delicate woven fabric), the 'tester' covering a four-poster bed and the 'toga' that covered the Romans. By the Middle Ages, 'thak', and later 'thatch', had emerged in English for the kind of reed or rush covering given a cottage to protect those within. 'Thug' took a different route.

Active in India for over four hundred years until their eradication in 1830, the Thuggee cult claimed to have killed over two million travellers to please their dark deity, the multi-armed Kali, goddess of destruction. As their favourite ruse was to ingratiate themselves with a major caravan only to rise up and murder everyone in their sleep, they took their name from the cognate Sanskrit 'sthaga', one who hides or covers up their real motives or intentions.

TIDE and TIDDLY

The 'time and tide' that waits for no man does so tautologically in that the Middle English 'tide' meant 'time' and was used to denote the oceanic phenomena occurring at specific times; this 'tide' was a distant relative of the German 'Zeit', as in 'Zeitgeist', the spirit or mood of the time. The links between 'time' and 'tide' is still visible in 'tidings', up-to-the-minute news; 'Whitsuntide', the time of Whitsun, or White Sunday; and phrases such as 'woe betide you'.

Through the notion of everything, such as the oceanic tides, being on time and in the right place, 'tidy' emerged in the fourteenth century to describe pleasing physical appearance or good health; it was not until the nineteenth century that it acquired overtones of presenting a neat array. That original meaning still appears in expressions such as 'a tidy income'.

To put things in tidy order was to 'tidivate' them, a term now presenting as 'titivate', and connections made between neatness and compactness produced 'tiddly', which expanded into 'tiddlywinks' for the game played with small counters that 'winked' or flipped in play; the name of the game was also taken as rhyming slang for 'drink', hence 'tiddly' for 'drunk'.

TOMBOLA and TUMBRIL

The common link is the French 'tomber', to fall, whence 'tumble', with the game developing in southern Italy before spreading throughout nineteenth-century Europe. As in the present form of bingo, the balls or tokens bearing the players' numbers were tumbled around in a barrel to ensure fair play before the winning numbers were drawn. As for 'bingo' itself, this is first noted as an eighteenth-century name for a heady mix of 'brandy' and 'stingo', a very strong ale that was supposed to put you on your feet again after a night on the tiles; perhaps, through associations with liveliness, the term shifted to the animated game.

As for the 'tumbril' or 'tumbrel' used to draw the condemned to their place of execution, this was named for its main purpose of hauling away that which 'tumbled out' of the rear end of livestock, such a cart being chosen for this final journey to heighten the humiliation of the condemned, who, clearly in serious trouble, were also said to be 'in the cart'.

TORPEDO and TORPOR

The Latin 'torpor' denoted a state of sluggish numbness, so the electric ray (fish) used in Roman medicine was called the 'torpedo', as those with epilepsy were induced to place their feet on such a creature in a crude form of electrotherapy, which naturally left them in a state of stunned torpor. In the 1770s the British Navy used the term for barrels of gunpowder set afloat with a slow fuse and left to drift into enemy shipping on which they had an equally stunning effect, the term surviving to make the transfer to the 'tin fish'-type torpedo designed by British engineer Robert Whitehead in the 1870s. Further refinements were made to Whitehead's brainchild by his son-in-law, the World War I Austrian submarine ace Ritter (not Baron) Georg von Trapp, who, with his second wife, Maria, went on to lesser things.

TRIVIA and OBVIOUS

The Roman crossroads only ever involved a meeting of three roads: one main, continuing thoroughfare intersected by two minor ones that terminated at the junction. Matters of importance were discussed in the fora and the Senate by men who dismissed the gossip of the homo-in-the-via, exchanged at street corners, as 'tri-via'.

'Obvious' originally denoted a road that was clear ahead, 'impervious' denoted one that was blocked, while a 'deviation' takes you away from your planned route.

TROPHY and TROPICAL

Usually made of captured enemy weapons, the Ancient Greeks built their 'trophies' on the battlefield at the point at which they felt events had turned in their favour, so naming them from 'trope', a turn. Later, when they brought home treasures in triumph, the term transferred. The 'tropics' mark the turning point of the sun and the boundaries beyond which the weather patterns take a turn, and terms such as 'apostrophe', the turned punctuation mark, and the 'heliotrope', the flower that always turns its face to the sun, are also allied terms.

TWAT and WHITTLE

Popular throughout most of the English-speaking world, 'twat' has been known since the early 1600s and is rooted in the Old Norse 'thveit', a cut, slit or clearing. Absorbed into English, this produced the synonymous 'thwat' and the rural 'twatchylle' or 'twatch', a 'bushy hole' left in a hedge by livestock forcing their way from one field to another – the allusions of 'twat' could hardly be made clearer. On a more respectable front, such terms also produced 'thwaite' to describe a forest clearing. Whilst it may not be difficult to see how we get from a bushy hole in a hedge to the present application of 'twat', it must be said that the term occupies a special place in publishing lore after its misuse by two prominent writers.

Vanity of Vanities (1660), possibly by Sir Henry Vane the Younger, includes the pitfall lines: 'They talked of his having a Cardinal's hat/They'd send him as soon an old nun's twat.' Here 'nun' presents the old synonym for 'prostitute', so when Shakespeare's Hamlet tells Ophelia, 'Get thee to a nunnery', he is *perhaps* not suggesting she try the cloistered life. Anyway, this left Robert Browning with the impression that 'twat' was an archaic term for a nun's headdress, so in *Pippa Passes* (1841) he talks of monks in cowls and nuns with their twats on their heads: 'Cowls and twats, monks and nuns in a cloister's moods.' When he realised his error Browning doubtless felt like a complete wimple.

Exactly thirty years later, 'twat' struck again. Lord Lytton's *The Coming Race* (1871) was a satire on Darwinism in which the author made much of a highly evolved super-race living on a magic fluid he called Vril, a term later hijacked for the trade name Bovril. At one point in the book a character admonishes his minions: 'Humble yourselves, my descendants. The father of your race was a twat.' Apparently Lytton though this the scientific term for a male tadpole.

TWILIGHT and TWEED

The Middle English 'two', 'twa' and 'twei' all meant the same, with 'twilight' the part of day that falls 'between' the two states of daylight and night. 'Twelve' carries a meaning of one complete batch of ten and two left over, and the 'twig' on a tree marks the division of new growth where the branch splits in two; 'twig' meaning 'to catch on' comes from the Irish 'twuigim', I understand. 'Twist' is cognate as it originally described the making of 'twine' from two threads, and 'betwixt' describes a midpoint between two options, as indeed does 'between', so 'betwixt and between' is definitely a tautology.

As for 'tweed', a spin-off from the double-woven 'tweel', this came about by accident. In 1830 the London tailors James Locke and Company received a consignment of such fabric from William Watson & Sons of Hawick in Scotland, but with the handwriting on the delivery note worthy of any doctor, the receiving clerk misread 'tweel' as 'tweed'. Thinking this evocative of the famous Scottish river, Lockes registered the term as a trade name, and although the tale smacks of the apocryphal, it gets a firm nod from the *OED*.

The final cognate of 'twain' was of course made famous by American writer Samuel Langhorne Clemens, who, passionate about the Mississippi and its riverboats, took his pen name from the call of the men who stood calmly 'swinging the lead' at the prow to take depth soundings. The line only had three markers and 'Mark twain!', the middle one, indicated a safe two fathoms.

TYRE and ATTIRE

The original and proper spelling of 'tyre' was 'tire'; *The Times* was perhaps the last champion of 'tire', finally and famously hanging up its gloves in 1931 with an editorial announcing it was to abandon its Canute-like opposition to the rising tide of 'tyre' and would thenceforth follow suit, no matter how wrong it was. Actually they were wrong about Canute, for he did not in fact try and order back the tides but rather went to the shore to show his sycophantic courtiers that his powers were limited, no matter their insane flatteries.

Long before it applied to rubber car tyres, the 'tire' was a metal ring that was heated and then shrink-fitted to wooden carriage wheels, with the term deriving either from 'attire', as in the final dressing of the wheel, or from 'tie-ring'. From the fifteenth to the seventeenth centuries the two spellings were used indiscriminately, but then 'tyre' fell from grace, leaving 'tire' to reign supreme, as indeed it does in America; the seat of English saw a comeback of 'tyre' in the nineteenth century.

U & V

VAMP and AVANT-GARDE

In the heyday of cavalry the 'avant-garde' – whence 'vanguard' – was the detachment riding in 'advance' of the column to scout for enemy or ambush, but as horse-soldiery started to give way to mechanised transport in the early twentieth century, the term shifted to those at the forefront of a fashion or trend. To the cobbler the 'avant-pied', or 'vamp', was the front upper of a shoe which could be replaced to 'revamp' footwear; as early as 1789 the term was adopted by musicians to mean 'extemporising' or 'vamping', as in 'revamping' a tune through the ad-lib reworking of the notes.

As applied to a woman exuding fatal attraction, 'vamp' is a truncation of 'vampire' that came into great use through the publicity surrounding a Broadway production of Porter

Emerson Browne's *A Fool There Was* (1909), the title taken from the opening line of Kipling's poem 'The Vampire', whose plot likewise centred on the activities of a woman who is certainly an emotional vampire and possibly a real one to boot. Famous for the line 'Kiss me, you fool', the play was turned into a silent film with Thea Bada playing The Vampire. In Hollywood's first-ever publicity stunt, a spurious biography was concocted for Bada, claiming that she was the orphan of an Arab sheik and a Frenchwoman who had been born in a tent in the Sahara. Further in keeping with this tosh, it was pointed out that her name was an anagram of 'Arab death'. Either way, Bada was forever after 'The Vamp', a term that still runs synonymous with 'femme fatale'.

VENTRILOQUISM and VENTRICLE

Magicians have always adopted contemporary religious rites and expressions to jazz up their acts, with 'magic' itself deriving from the Magi, the mystic priests who visited the two-year-old Jesus in 'the house', Matthew 1:11 – they were not present at the Nativity scene. 'Hocus pocus' is a scrambling of 'hoc est corpus', as intoned in the consecration of the Mass, and 'abracadabra' but a mumbling of the Ancient Aramaic 'Abhadda kedabrah!' – disappear (sickness) as this word (is spoken) – as used by early religious healers.

Likewise, 'ventriloquism' is just a reworking of an old ruse employed by pagan priests. Deriving from the Latin 'venter', a stomach, and 'loqui', speak, prophets and seers of Ancient

Greece and Rome commonly employed the trick of standing, mouth agape as if in a trance, to allow the spirits residing in their stomachs to utter prophesies. Still spouting religio-prophetic mumbo-jumbo, ventriloquising charlatans were popular acts from medieval times onwards; in 1886 Fred Russell and his dummy (from 'dumb'), Coster Joe, appeared at London's Palace Theatre and for the first time presented the skill as one of entertainment only.

From the first element of 'venter' there also derives the 'ventricle' of the heart, seen as a little stomach for blood, and 'ventral' to denote anything associated with the abdomen, especially breathing or laughter, both of which cause the stomach to rise and fall. In the nineteenth century, 'ventral laugh' denoted the silent, stifled kind that is only shown in the shaking belly, but when the expression was updated to 'belly laugh' at the start of the twentieth century, this was mistakenly applied to open and full laughter.

VERONICA and ICONOCLAST

Both produced by the Greek 'eikon', an image or portrait, with 'iconoclast' produced by the tacking on of a suffix derived from 'klastes', one who breaks. This same second element is present in 'pyroclastic' flow, the wave of searing hot gas that, during a volcanic eruption, can race ahead of the lava flow at speeds of 500 mph, smashing everything in its path.

Christian tradition has it that when Jesus was on way to his crucifixion a woman stepped from the crowd; after mopping the sweat from his face, she found the image of his features indelibly etched into her cloth, this earning her the name of 'Veronica', which basically means the 'vera' (true) image. In the unpleasant spectacle of bullfighting, 'veronica' describes the matador's ploy of standing still to wipe the cape across the face of the passing bull.

VILLAGE and VILLAIN

The ultimate source is the Latin 'villaticum', a country estate, this entering English to produce both 'villa' and 'village'. To the Romans a 'villanus' was a low farmhand and doubtless a thief to boot, and it was with these overtones that 'villain' invaded English. The Roman villanus could also be a slave from any one of the nations under the Roman yoke, their offspring tending to speak a kind of pidgin Latin, so from 'vernaculus', a slave born on the master's property, we get 'in the vernacular'.

This notion of our country cousins being no better than they should be is reflected in 'pagan' and 'heathen', the former deriving from the Latin 'pagus', the countryside, and the second simply denoting a dweller of the heath. Conversely, if you lived in a city – or 'urbs', as it was in Latin – you were 'urbane', and as a city-dweller was a 'civis', only city-dwellers could be 'civilians', 'civil' of manner or 'civilised'.

The 'villain' charged with the responsibility of maintaining all the fires in a house was nicknamed 'blackguard' and was rarely paid in anything other than food and shelter. Any blackguards who needed a bob or three to buy some of life's little comforts had to go a-mugging at night, this nocturnal activity leading 'blackguard' to its present position in English.

VIRAGO and WEREWOLF

The common root here is 'vir', Latin for 'man', and while this meaning is clear in terms such as 'virile', there was a most decidedly sexist agendum behind the development of allied terms.

According to the Romans, only a man could hold 'virtue' or acquire sufficient skill in any one metier to be considered a 'virtuoso'; 'virgin' denoted a woman lacking a man and, speak it not within the portals of a certain publishing house, but 'virago' denoted a brave and heroic woman, almost good enough to be a man – but not quite.

Through the well-established shift from V to W there emerged 'were' to name the 'werewolf', or man-wolf.

VULGAR and MOB

The Middle Latin 'vulgus' denoted the general people, with 'vulgar' appearing in English at the close of the fourteenth century, to mean 'pertaining to the ordinary people'. This meaning is still visible in ordinary fractions being termed vulgar fractions and the everyday version of the Bible being termed the Vulgate. Perhaps inevitably, elitism showed its ugly face, and by the mid-1700s overtones of coarseness and crudity had asserted themselves. A cognate is 'divulge', which originally meant 'to make something known to the masses'.

'Mob', a truncation of 'mobile vulgus', the Latin equivalent of 'the madding crowd', entered English towards the close of the seventeenth century and went straight downmarket to describe a group of common people united in criminal intent. The only respectability the term has ever enjoyed is as a collective noun for kangaroos. In nineteenth-century America, 'the Mob' denoted the oldest of the American criminal fraternities – the Irish Mob. The designation has never properly applied to the Mafia, which still prefers to be known as 'Cosa Nostra' (Our Thing).

WHIP and VIBRATOR

Etymologically speaking, 'whip' and 'vibrator' lie in the same bed, deriving as they do from the Middle Latin 'vibrare', to shake, but also understood to mean 'alive' or 'lively', as in 'vibrant'. The 'viper' took its name for giving birth to live young instead of laying eggs, which is something of a rarity in snake-world. The 'whip', meanwhile, certainly makes the idle look lively and the canine 'whippet' is a lively runner.

As for the much-put-upon 'whipping boy', this was once a proper job title. Throughout the sixteenth and seventeenth centuries, the Divine Right of Kings meant that nobody could lay hand on either the king or his son, who were revered as God-appointed rulers. Bizarre as it may sound now, every prince had a whipping boy for the teacher to beat in his stead should he make a Horlicks of his Latin homework. The upside for the whipping boy was a first-class education, and many made lasting friendships; Charles I elevated his whipping boy, William Murray, to the peerage as the First Earl of Dysart, complete with palatial residence and lands.

WITHERS and WITHSTAND

'With' does not mean 'in unison' but rather 'against' or 'in opposition', so the politicians' cry of 'Are you with me?' is in fact asking the audience to vote for the opposition. A horse's 'withers', located on top of the shoulders, appear to the rider to be fighting against each other as the animal moves along. The proper meaning of 'with' is perhaps clearer in terms such as 'withstand', 'withhold' and 'withershins', as said of anything turning the wrong way, or fighting against the norm.

It was talk of people arguing 'with' each other or fighting 'with' each other that gradually introduced the sense of togetherness that became generally accepted by the early sixteenth century.

YODEL and JUBILEE

The Ancient Hebrew calendar ran on shmitas, blocks of seven years, and after seven shmitas, or forty-nine years, every fiftieth year was marked by relaxation and celebration. As explained in Leviticus, 25:9–18, the land was allowed to lie fallow; all wars were suspended and the army stood down; all slaves were freed and no planting was allowed. The commencement of this year was announced by military heralds riding from town to town, blowing on their 'yobels', bugles made from a ram's horn, and it was a short step from 'yobelee' to 'jubilee'. In military circles, 'yobel' could also denote a battering ram, so the yarn of Joshua at the walls of Jericho might indeed be built on some kernel of truth, with the walls falling not to trumpet blasts but to battering rams.

Obviously jubilee year was marked with much 'jubilation' and the Medieval Latin 'jubilare' arrived in German as 'jodelen', whence the Tyrolean torture known as 'yodelling'.

YOGA and CONJUGAL

Both of these suggest a joining together, with the former taken directly from the Sanskrit term for a joining or yoking, the term adopted for its ethos of seeing mental and physical health as inexorably united. The 'conjugal' bliss hopefully enjoyed by a man and woman 'yoked' in marriage is thus clear, but perhaps less so 'jugular' as descriptive of the veins joining the head and body. There are in fact four jugulars, two interior and two anterior, which makes nonsense of anyone talking of 'going for the jugular'. Another obvious use appears in the 'yoke' of oxen and the 'yokel' leading them.

ZANY and YANKEE

Despite the decidedly modern sound of 'zany' and its adoption into the jargon of the hippy movement of the 1960s, the term had been in use since the 1500s. The Italian equivalent of 'John' was and still is 'Giovanni'; in the Venetian dialect this was commonly shortened to 'Gianni', with the G pronounced as a J, this further corrupting to 'Zuan' and 'Zanni', both of which should be pronounced as if the Z were a soft J. It was this latter form that was taken as the name of the stock buffoon in the Venetian commedia dell'arte. 'Zany' fell from common usage in the UK but survived in America due to the significant Italian presence in that country. When reimported in the 1960s through American television programmes – most notably *Rowan & Martin's Laugh-In*, which featured a very young Goldie Hawn as a decidedly off-the-wall and dizzy blonde – 'zany' was embraced in the UK by a new generation that had never before heard the usage.

In previous centuries most European nations had nicknames for each other, these invariably featuring the name John – as explained elsewhere in this book 'Johnny Toad' was the English name for the French, who retaliated with 'Jean Boule', Johnny Liar, a name quite in keeping with their concept of Perfidious Albion. 'Jean Boule' was heard with misplaced pride by the English as John Bull, a concept on which John Arbuthnot built a national identity in 1712, unaware of the muffled sniggering across the Channel. The French influence into the Southern American states ensured a place for 'boule' but it was again misunderstood by non-French speakers who, hearing it as 'bull', added 'shit' as an intensifier for verbal rubbish. And to most, a Dutchman was 'Johnny Cheese' (Jan Kaas, pronounced 'Kees').

In the form of 'Yankey', that same jibe is first noted in 1683 when it was being used by the English to describe the Dutch freebooters operating off the coast of what is now called New England but was then New Holland. By extension it was next applied to the Dutch settlers of New Amsterdam – later New York – who, adopting the term themselves, turned it on their adversaries, the English settlers of Connecticut to their north, thought by the Dutch to be too clever for their own good; they would later be personified as the lead character in Mark Twain's *A Connecticut Yankee in King Arthur's Court* (1889). It was most likely the native population of America who, indifferent to the country of origin of their collective invaders, applied 'Yankee' willy-nilly to any white person. Eventually, the term was bandied as an insult by one and all in the Northern States, leading its adoption by the breakaway South as a term for any denizen of the North.

The notion of a Yankee being slick and cunning remains in the pump screwdriver that bears the name, and also in the complicated multiple bet laid at the bookies.

ZAP and SAPPER

For all its modern and onomatopoeic sound, 'zap' is not a modernism from twentieth-century American comics but instead a medieval Italian term. The *OED* presents a quote from 1600 demanding that the castle ramparts be 'zapped', as derived from the Italian 'zappere', to inflict damage with explosives. The charges were dug in against the walls by the 'zapper', a title entering English as 'sapper'. Thus the Italians have been talking about 'zapping' people and places for centuries and it is perhaps not too difficult to figure out which particular group of Italian 'businessmen' put 'zap' into American slang as meaning 'to kill an individual'.